ENGLISH

MATTERS

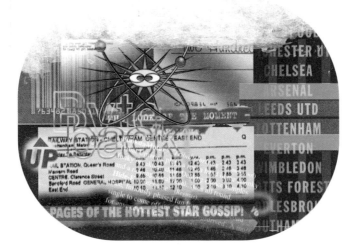

SUSAN DUBERLEY

Heinemann

Contents

Throughout this book you will find the following cross-references

TRF PAGES 00–00	There are specific activities or notes in the Teacher's File which relate to the activity
SKILLS PAGES 00–00	The skills section offers practice in the skills you need for the activity
SEE ALSO PAGES 00–00	Other pages in the book will help you with the activity

Out and about

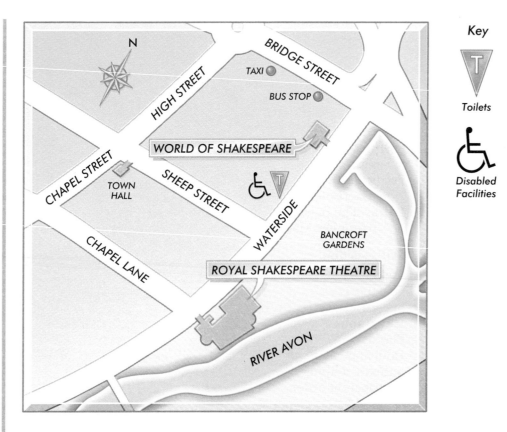

1.1

Look at the map above, then answer the questions below.

1 You get off at the bus stop in Bridge Street. Describe how to get to:
a) the World of Shakespeare
b) the Royal Shakespeare Theatre.

2 Describe how you get from the Royal Shakespeare Theatre to:
a) the Town Hall   *b)* the taxi rank.

3 Give directions from the Town Hall to:
a) the toilets   *b)* the taxi rank.

4 Can the toilets on Waterside be used by disabled people?

5 Where might you be able to sit on a sunny day and have a picnic?

1.2

Look at the bus timetable, then answer the questions below.

OXFORD – CHIPPING NORTON – STRATFORD

MONDAY TO SATURDAY (EXCEPT PUBLIC HOLIDAYS)

	Morning			
Operator:	T	T	O	T
Service No:	20A	20C	X50	20A
OXFORD	8.05	8.30	9.15	9.30
YARNTON	8.22	....	....	9.47
BEGBROKE	8.27	8.46	9.33	9.52
WOODSTOCK	8.35	8.52	9.40	9.58

OPERATOR CODES: O = The Oxford Bus Company
                                        T = Thames Transit

Service No – service number

1 *a)* What time is the first bus from Oxford to Woodstock?
   b) What number would be on the front of this bus?
   c) Which bus company is being used for this journey?
   d) How long does this bus take to get from Oxford to Woodstock?

2 You want to get to Yarnton after nine o'clock.
   What time does the bus leave Oxford?

3 You catch the 9.15 bus from Oxford.
   a) Which bus company will be taking you?
   b) What will be the number of the bus?

Listen to the instructions in the Teacher's File.

1.3

TRF
PAGE 15

NOW EXPRESS YOURSELF

Congratulations, you're there!
Now how are you getting home?

Simple. A student coachcard from National
Express – it's your passport to easy travel.
Costing just £20 and valid for three whole
years (or £8 for one year), you'll never have
to worry about getting to and from home, or
making any other trips while you're a student.

As a card holder, you'll get discounts of up
to 30% off standard fares on any National
Express coach. Chances are, you'll cover the
cost of your card on your first few journeys.

So how do you get it?
All you need is a passport-sized
photograph – then
complete the
application form
on this leaflet.

DISCOUNT COACHCARD
CARD TYPE STUDENT
30TH SEPT 1997
NAME ALISON WILD
Card No. K 010648

TYPICAL SAVINGS			
Journey	Normal Adult Economy Return	Discount Fare	£ Saving
London – Birmingham	£14.75	£10.50	£4.25
London – Nottingham	£19.00	£13.50	£5.50
Manchester – Bournemouth	£37.00	£26.00	£11.00
Oxford – Cambridge	£15.50	£11.25	£4.25
Newcastle – Plymouth	£59.50	£42.00	£17.50

Fares are correct as at May 1996. Please enquire for correct fare for your journey. Fares are subject to change without notice.

> **valid** – can be used
> **discount** – money has been taken off
> **standard** – usual
> **subject to change** – can be changed

1.4

Study the details on the opposite page and then answer these questions.

1 Which coach company is making this offer?

2 How long can you go on using the £20 student coachcard?

3 If you only wanted a student coachcard for a year, how much would it cost?

4 Why would a student want a student coachcard?

5 What do you have to do in order to get a student coachcard?

6 *a)* What is the cost of an ordinary coach ticket from Newcastle to Plymouth?
  b) What is the cost of the same journey if you have a student coachcard?
  c) How much money have you saved by owning a student coachcard?

7 When were the details of the coach fares printed?

8 What should you do to be sure that the coach fares are the same as those given on this leaflet?

9 What does the leaflet say that the coach company can do at any time?

1.5

SKILLS
PAGE 119

On October 14th you travelled by National Express from Newcastle to Portsmouth. When you arrived at college you realised you had left one of your travel bags in the coach. Write a letter to the company to ask if your bag has been found.

◆ Describe the bag and where you were sitting, and give any other information you think might be important.

◆ Their address is: National Express, Newcastle upon Tyne NE29 8RN.

The Red Lion Hotel

TARIFF CARD
(effective from 1st April 1996)

BED AND BREAKFAST	All rates are per person per night	BARGAIN BREAK
£43.00	Single Room	£56.50
£35.00	Twin/Double Room	£48.50
£50.00	Double Room for Single Person	£62.50
Includes: Accommodation, full English Breakfast and VAT	All rooms have en suite bathrooms, colour TV, radio, telephone, coffee/tea making facilities. Car park to the rear of Hotel. Ground floor rooms suitable for guests with disabilities.	**Includes:** Accommodation, full English Breakfast, Evening Dinner and VAT **Note: Minimum Stay = 2 days**

BONUS DAYS

LOW SEASON: November, December, January, February
Book two days – **stay third free**

EARLY SEASON: March, April, May, June, July
Book two days – **stay third at half price**

HIGH SEASON: August, September, October
Book six days – **stay seventh free**

Note: Excludes Bank Holiday weekends, Christmas and New Year

Dogs: ONLY BY PRIOR ARRANGEMENT and at an extra charge of £3 per night to cover additional cleaning of room. Dogs must not be left in the room unattended.

effective from the 1st of April – starts on this date
per – each
accommodation – a place to stay, live
VAT – **V**alue **A**dded **T**ax, a tax that is sometimes added to a bill
en suite – connected with, forming a unit
minimum – the smallest amount
prior – before

1.6

Look at the details about the Red Lion Hotel, then answer the questions below.

1 How much would it cost to stay for one night in a single room with bed and breakfast?

2 What extra do you get if you have a bargain break?

3 How long do you have to stay at the Red Lion to be able to get a bargain break?

4 How much a day would it cost if you were staying in a single room but had the bargain break?

5 You want to stay at the Red Lion but all the single rooms are booked. How much would it cost you to stay one night for bed and breakfast in a double room on your own?

6 Under what conditions can you stay at the Red Lion free, for one day?

7 At which times of the year are bonus days not on offer?

8 In what way might the hotel be suitable for someone in a wheelchair?

9 If you want to bring a dog, what must you do first?

10 Draw and label a diagram to show single room accommodation at the Red Lion. Show the position of the bed and the other room facilities.

1.7

Listen to the talk in the Teacher's File.

TRF
PAGE 20–22

WHAT'S ON

ROLLER SKATING

Tedley Skating Rink,
Chalford End

BANK HOLIDAY SPECIAL

**Open all day
9 a.m. to 11 p.m.**

**9 a.m. to 3 p.m.:
Family Special.**
£5 for 2 adults
& 2 children
(inclusive of skate hire)

**9 p.m. to 11 p.m.:
Night Special.**
£3 for 2 adults
including skate hire.

Enjoy yourself the skating way
ALL DAY

The Birds of Prey Centre

Tedley Park Centre, Charn Way, Tedley
Tel: 01907 693205

Don't miss this Bank Holiday Display.
Watch eagles, hawks,
and falcons in a 45 minute
flying display.

**11 a.m., 1 p.m.,
3 p.m. and 5 p.m.**

Enjoy our Hawk Walk,
picnic areas and coffee and
gift shops. Free Parking.
♿ Disabled welcome. No pets
Adults £3.50. Children £2.50

THIS BANK HOLIDAY

The Country Centre, Hillcroft Road, Tedley
Phone: 01907 987654 for details of our
year round activities

MOUNTAIN BIKE OBSTACLE COURSE

Test your cycling
skills for £1
11 a.m. to 4.30 p.m

FAMILY TREASURE HUNT

Search the woods for
hidden treasure
£3 per family
11 a.m. to 4 p.m.

inclusive of skate hire – the cost of hiring skates is
included in the price

obstacles – things that get in the way.

1.8

**Read the advertisements on page 10, then answer the
questions below.**

1 What sort of holiday is it?

2 Why is it a test of skills to
go on The Mountain Bike
Obstacle Course?

3 What other activity can you
do at the Country Centre?

4 How long do the flying
displays last at the
Birds of Prey Centre?

5 What does this sign mean?

6 Why do you think you must
not bring pets to the
Birds of Prey Centre?

7 Do people using the Family
Special skating time need to
bring their own roller skates
to use the skating rink?
How do you know?

8 *a)* Which of these activities
would you most like to go
to? Say why.

b) If you would not like to
go to any of these, say
where you would like to
go and why.

1.9

TRF
PAGE 11

OPTIONS

1 Give a talk about an activity you are interested in or have
enjoyed. Think about how to make your talk interesting to the
group.

2 *a)* Write a brief report about the entertainments that are going
to take place over the Bank Holiday in Tedley. Your report
is to be used for a 30 second spot on your local radio.
Use the events on page 10. Add other events if you like.

b) Read your report out loud. Remember to speak clearly and
slowly.

IDEAL SLEEPING PARTNERS: The female scorpion with a dozen youngsters on her back found in the sleeping bag.

1.10

Read the article on page 13, then answer these questions.

1 Where was Stephen staying for his holiday?

2 Where was his home?

3 What made Stephen think there was something in his sleeping bag?

4 What did he do when he found out that it was a scorpion?

5 How do you know that the scorpion was female?

6 How did the scorpion get into the sleeping bag?

7 What has happened to the scorpion now?

8 What would you do if you found a scorpion in your sleeping bag?

9 Would you mind having your photograph and your story in the local newspaper? Give your reasons.

Steve's bedfellow had a sting in her tail

by LAURA JOINT

HOLIDAYMAKER Stephen Savva had the shock of his life when he woke up in his sleeping bag and found a scorpion crawling on his neck.

Stephen, 14, discovered his creepy bedfellow when he felt something tickle him, and when he got up, he spotted an insect looking snug in his sleeping bag.

Londoner Stephen, who is on holiday in Teignmouth this week, kept his wits about him and put the scorpion in a jar.

The teenager, who is staying with his friend Dane Ramshaw at Dane's grandmother's house, actually had a lucky escape – the scorpion later gave birth to more than a dozen babies.

Painful

Mother and baby scorpions are now doing well at Shaldon Wildlife Trust, which has agreed to look after them.

Stephen said yesterday: "I was shocked more than anything when I saw it. It was about three inches long.

"I have been told that it was a European Scorpion. We think it must have crept into the sleeping bag when my brother was coming back from holiday in France.

"I was lucky. They can give you quite a nasty sting."

IN THE BAG: Stephen Savva with the sleeping bag he shared with a pregnant scorpion.

Adapted from *The Western Morning News*

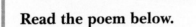

1.11

Read the poem below.

Coming home on my own

I slept with fourteen strange
people, in the youth hostel room.
All of us had to get up early.
I turned and opened my eyes –
5 it was bright open daylight.
Right away everybody turned over
too, woke up, began to talk.
And it was good how we washed,
dressed and made breakfast together.
10 But we broke up. We separated
on foot, on bicycles
and I by bus – waving good-bye.

James Berry

1.12

Answer these questions about the poem.

1 The person in the poem was on holiday. What kind of holiday was it?

2 What were the best things about the holiday?

3 *a)* How do you think the person felt at the end of the poem?
   b) Why do you think the person felt this way?

4 How would you feel if you had the same kind of experience?

Fit to eat

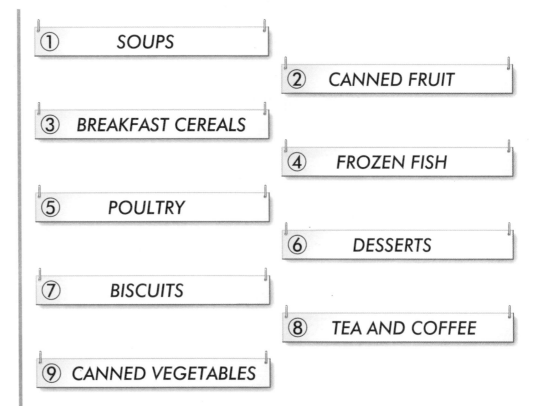

① SOUPS

② CANNED FRUIT

③ BREAKFAST CEREALS

④ FROZEN FISH

⑤ POULTRY

⑥ DESSERTS

⑦ BISCUITS

⑧ TEA AND COFFEE

⑨ CANNED VEGETABLES

2.1

1–9 are signs in a supermarket.
Write down where you would go to get the foods below (e.g. a = 8)

a) a packet of tea

b) cornflakes

c) tinned tomatoes

d) chocolate biscuits

e) fish fingers

f) a turkey

g) baked beans

h) vegetable soup

i) a tin of pears

j) cod in batter

k) jelly

l) a chicken

NOT TOO FAT

NOT TOO THIN

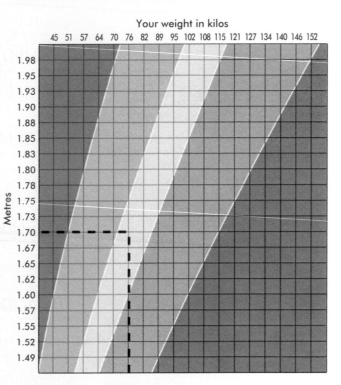

Your weight in kilos

	Underweight
Maybe you need to eat a bit more. But go for well-balanced, nutritious foods and don't just fill up on fatty and sugary foods.

| | OK |
You're eating the right quantity of food but you need to be sure that you're getting a healthy balance in your diet.

| | Overweight |
You should try to lose weight.

| | Fat |
You need to lose weight.

| | Very Fat |
You urgently need to lose weight. You would do well to see a doctor.

For example, a person who is 1.70 metres tall and weighs 76 kilos is overweight.

well-balanced meals – meals which have a mixture of different sorts of foods

nutritious foods – foods that are good for you

2.2

Read the details on page 16, then answer the questions below.

1 What colour on the graph stands for a person who is just the right weight?

2 What colour on the graph stands for someone who is underweight?

3 *a)* Work out if the two people below are the right weight or not.
   i) Person A is 1.78 metres tall and weighs 51 kilos.
   ii) Person B is 1.60 metres tall and weighs 108 kilos.

   b) Using the details given on the opposite page, explain in your own words what Person A should eat.

   c) What two things should Person B do?

4 What is the advice given to someone who is just the right weight?

MY TV DINNER
IMELDA STAUNTON

Appears in BBC2's
'Look at the State We're In' on Saturday

I wouldn't eat a wonderful meal while watching TV because it would be a waste of good food. A simple meal is a big bowl of my home-made vegetable casserole – I'm a vegetarian – followed by any sort of ice-cream. Both can be eaten with a spoon, so I don't miss the programme while cutting up the food, and I sit in a very short rocking-chair with a cushion on my lap and three cats watching me.

Adapted from *The Radio Times*

vegetarian – someone who does not eat meat

2.3 Read 'My TV Dinner' above, then answer these questions.

1 Who wrote 'My TV Dinner'?

2 Why did the writer want to eat with a spoon?

3 Write down where each detail in the picture can be found, e.g. bowl – line 3.

4 Which magazine did 'My TV Dinner' come from?

5 Why are some people vegetarians? Do you agree with them?

2.4 Write your own 'TV Dinner'.

HOW TO MAKE CUSTARD

Using the pictures below, write the instructions on how to make custard. You should number your instructions 1–6.

The instructions are to go on the label of a tin of custard powder.

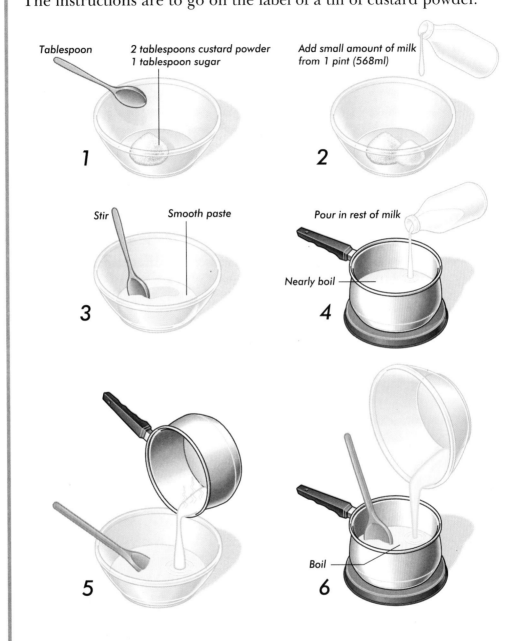

Tablespoon · 2 tablespoons custard powder / 1 tablespoon sugar · 1

Add small amount of milk from 1 pint (568ml) · 2

Stir · Smooth paste · 3

Pour in rest of milk · Nearly boil · 4

5

Boil · 6

2.6

TRF
PAGE 28

Now compare what you have done with the instructions on a tin of custard.

Instructions appear in the Teacher's File on page 28.

Say which parts are better and why.

- Is there more detail?
- Is it better explained?

TIPS FOR A BACTERIA-FREE BARBECUE

It's the ideal summer. Sunny weather, a few friends and that rich and smoky smell of the barbecue. But although eating outdoors sounds fun, you can get food poisoning if you do not follow safety rules.

One of the main problems is that people just do not cook their food for long enough. The outside of the food looks ready but the inside isn't, and that leads to many cases of food poisoning. So here are some tips to keep you safe.

- Put food in the fridge or a cool bag with icepacks until it is needed.

- Anything which is thick or has bones should be cooked slowly in the oven first, then finished off on the barbecue, so that it will still have that smoky flavour.

- If food starts to burn on the outside during cooking, raise the grill or reduce the heat of the coals, so the food has time to cook on the inside.

- Take care to cook until the juices run clear. Under-cooked burgers, sausages and poultry can be a serious hazard.

- Eat the food as soon as it is ready.

- Keep raw and cooked meats apart and don't handle cooked foods with utensils that have touched raw meats.

Adapted from *The Western Mail*

to reduce – to lower, cut down
hazard – a danger
utensils – cooking tools, e.g. knives, forks, prongs

2.7

Read the leaflet on page 20, then answer the questions.

1 What is this leaflet about?

2 *a)* What is a common cause of food poisoning?
b) Write down TWO tips that can prevent this from happening.

3 How could you make sure you did not touch raw and cooked foods with the same utensils?

4 You are planning to have a picnic barbecue away from home. How can you keep the raw food fresh before you use it?

OPTIONS

2.8

A group of you are helping to put on a barbecue to raise money for charity. The barbecue is on Saturday 28th July. It is to be held in the Gladthorpe playing fields and begins at 7 o'clock at night. There is to be a raffle and other money-raising activities.

SKILLS
PAGE 119

1 Write a letter to Hortley Stores asking them if they would like to make a donation towards the charity. Use your own name and address. Decide which charity you are hoping to raise money for. The store is in West Street, Gladthorpe.

SKILLS
PAGES 120–121

2 You bought a packet of sausages from Hortley Stores for the barbecue. You find they have mould on them. Write a letter of complaint to Hortley Stores Head Office, PO Box 297, Westbrook Trading Estate, Canterbury CT6 4GD. Use the details above and your own address.

The coach rattled away and left only a cloud of dust behind

2.9

Oliver Twist is ten. Both of his parents are dead. He has been working for an unkind and cruel man and cannot stand it any longer. In the extract below, Oliver is running away. Read the extract.

Oliver walked twenty miles that day and all that time tasted nothing but the crust of bread, and a few draughts of water, which he begged at the cottage-doors by the roadside. When the night came, he turned into a meadow; and creeping close under a hayrick, determined to lie there till morning. He felt frightened at first for the wind moaned dismally over the empty fields, and he was cold and hungry, and more alone than he'd ever felt before. Being very tired with his walk, however, he soon fell asleep and forgot his troubles.

He felt cold and stiff when he got up next morning, and so hungry that he was obliged to exchange the penny for a small loaf in the very first village he passed. He had walked no more than twelve miles, when night closed in again. His feet were sore, and his legs so weak that they trembled beneath him. Another night passed in the bleak damp air made him worse; when he set forward on his journey next morning, he could hardly crawl along.

He waited at the bottom of a steep hill till a stage coach came up, and then begged of the outside passengers; but there were very few who would take any notice of him; and even those told him to wait till they got to the top of the hill, and then let them see how far he could run for a half-penny. Poor Oliver tried to keep up with the coach a little way, but was unable to do it by reason of his fatigue and sore feet.

When the outsides saw this they put their half-pence back in their pockets again, declaring that he was an idle dog, and didn't deserve anything; and the coach rattled away and left only a cloud of dust behind.

In some villages, large painted boards were fixed up: warning all persons who begged within the district, that they would be sent to jail. This frightened Oliver very much, and made him glad to get out of those villages.

From *Oliver Twist* by Charles Dickens

draught – drink

meadow – field

hayrick – stack of hay (dried grass)

outside passengers – those passengers on top of the coach

fatigue – great tiredness

idle – lazy

2.10

Now answer these questions.

1 How far has Oliver walked in two days?

2 How much has Oliver had to eat in two days?

3 Read the first two paragraphs again.
   a) Write down four words that describe the state that Oliver was in.
   b) Write down three words that describe what the weather was like at night.

4 About how much money do you think a penny was worth in Oliver's time?

5 Explain in your own words:
   a) What did the people in the coach want Oliver to do before they would give him a half-penny?
   b) Why could Oliver not do what they wanted?
   c) What did the people in the coach think of Oliver?

6 How can you tell that there were quite a few people in Oliver's time who were hungry and poor?

UNIT 3

For sale

3.1

Read the advertisement below.

For Sale

BOY'S MOUNTAIN BIKE,

suit 5–8 yrs, blue/white vgc

£30 ono.

Tel: 0181 109 8765

---

yrs is short for years

vgc stands for **v**ery **g**ood **c**ondition

ono stands for **o**r **n**ear **o**ffer

Tel is short for telephone number

3.2 Write out the advertisement in full. Put the abbreviations into words. Use the notes opposite to help you.

3.3 Answer these questions about the bike.

1 What sort of bike is for sale?

2 How much does it cost?

3 What colour is the bike?

4 Mrs Chipeck is looking for a bike for Ann, aged ten. Would the bike make a good present? Say why.

5 Should you offer £30? Say why.

6 How could you find out more about the bike?

3.4 **OPTIONS**

1 You have seen an advertisement for a bike that you would like for yourself. Make a list of questions to ask when you phone up about it.

2 Describe something you would like to buy, for example a radio-controlled model aeroplane, or a camera. Give as much detail as you can. Say why you would like to have it.

MAKE MONEY FAST WITH

Herald & Post

CLASSIFIED ADVERTISING

ARTICLES UNDER £100 FREE

Simply fill in the coupon and send it to us at the address below to reach us by Monday 12 noon prior to publication

NO EXPENSIVE TELEPHONE LINES

Private Advertisers only
Not to be used for Motor or pets

ARTICLES FOR SALE
Sell it Fast

Name _____

Address _____

_____

_____

_____

_____

Tel _____

NORTHUMBERLAND/NORTH TYNESIDE
Herald & Post

36 Bridge Street, Morpeth NE61

noon – the middle of the day, 12 o'clock a.m.
prior – before

3.5

Read the advertisement opposite, then answer the questions below.

1 Which newspaper does the advertisement come from?

2 How much would it cost if you wanted to sell some trainers for £30, using the advertisement opposite?

3 How many words are you allowed to use when you write the details of what you want to sell? (You can have one word for each box.)

4 When you have filled out the coupon what should you do next?

5 If you want your **for sale** details in the newspaper this week, by when must the newspaper have your filled in coupon?

6 There are two things you cannot sell using this advertisement. What are they?

3.6

Think of something that you could sell, for example a doll's house, skateboard, posters. Write down the details that could go in the coupon opposite.

Strike a light!

GLOUCESTER collector Robert Opie, above, is thought to have set a new world record. He shelled out a staggering £4,100 at an auction for two empty matchboxes from the late 1820s.

Experts say the price was bigger than anything paid for a matchbox in Britain and is believed to be the biggest amount paid in the world.

Mr Opie admitted today that the price was 'absurd' but said he was delighted with his buy.

Match expert Pauline Lazarus said the boxes were the first labelled matchboxes in the world.

The matchboxes are not likely to go on display yet at the Robert Opie Packaging Museum in Gloucester Docks, but may appear as part of a special exhibition at a later date.

Slightly adapted from the *Forest Citizen*

auction – a sale where people call out (bid) how much they will pay. The person who calls out the highest sum of money gets the item
absurd – silly

3.7

Read the article opposite, then answer the questions below.

1 What was the name of the man who bought the matchboxes?

2 How much did he pay for the matchboxes?

3 When were the matchboxes made?

4 What was special about the matchboxes?

5 What did he want the matchboxes for?

6 Write down two words or phrases that highlight what a lot of money was spent on the matchboxes.

7 What other sorts of things do you think he has in his museum?

8 Why might people find the museum interesting?

3.8

TRF
PAGES 11

OPTIONS

1 Give a talk about a collection of your own. You could bring in some of the things you collect.

2 Write a newspaper article like the one opposite about your collection, or the collection of someone you know. Describe how a new item was found. Perhaps you or the person you know found a bargain in a jumble sale.

3 a) Make a list of some of the things that you could collect. Write down some of the ways you could get new items for your collection.
b) Now write a leaflet for ten-year-olds on 'Making a Collection'. Look at the leaflet on barbecue tips on page 20 for ideas on how to lay out your leaflet.

SEE ALSO
PAGE 20

4 Write a story or article about finding something in your loft that turns out to be worth a lot of money.

3.9

Read the following passage.

She was standing by the river looking at the stepping stones and
remembering each one. There was the round unsteady stone, the
pointed one, the flat one in the middle – the safe stone where you
could stand and look round. The next wasn't so safe, for when the
5 river was full the water flowed over it and even when it showed
dry it was slippery. But after that it was easy and soon
she was standing on the other side.

    The road was much wider than it used to be but the work had
been done carelessly. The felled trees had not been cleared away
10 and the bushes looked trampled. Yet it was the same road and
she walked along feeling extraordinarily happy.

    It was a fine day, a blue day. The only thing was that the sky
had a glassy look that she didn't remember. That was the only
word she could think of. Glassy. She turned the corner
15 and saw that the old pavement had been taken up, and there too
the road was much wider, but it had the same unfinished look.

    She came to the worn stone steps that led up to the house and
her heart began to beat. The screw pine was gone, so was the
mock summer house called the ajoupa, but the clove tree was
still there and at the top of the steps the rough lawn stretched
20 away, just as she remembered it. She stopped and looked
towards the house that had been added to and painted white.
It was strange to see a car standing in front of it.

    There were two children under the big mango tree, a boy and a
little girl, and she waved to them and called, "Hello," but they
25 didn't answer her or turn their heads . . .

The grass was yellow in the hot sunlight as she walked towards them. When she was quite close she called again, shyly: "Hello." Then, "I used to live here once," she said.

Still they didn't answer. When she said for the third time, "Hello," she was quite near them. Her arms went out with a longing to touch them.

It was the boy who turned. His grey eyes looked straight into hers. His expression didn't change. He said: "Hasn't it gone cold all of a sudden? D'you notice? Let's go in."

"Yes. Let's go in," said the girl.

Her arms fell to her sides as she watched them running across the grass to the house. That was the first time she knew.

Slightly adapted from *I used to live here once* by Jean Rhys

3.10

Answer the questions below.

1 The last line of the story is: 'That was the first time she knew.'
   a) What did she 'know'?
   b) How did she know? What had happened to make her realise?
   c) How do you think the children felt? Say why.

2 Write down the details in the story that make the reader feel that the woman is normal.

3 How does the woman feel about coming back to the house?

4 Why do you think the woman has come back to the house?

5 How does the woman feel at the end of the story? Why do you think she feels like this?

6 What are some of the things that might happen next?

3.11

OPTIONS

1 Write a diary entry from the point of view of one of the children in the story.

2 Write part of a scene from a play where two people think there is a ghost in the house.
   To see how a play should be set out, look out at 'Hurricane Dub', on pages 46–47.

SEE ALSO

PAGES 46–47

4 Heads and tails

4.1

The instructions 1–6 below are from a can of wasp and fly spray, but they are in the wrong order. Write down the numbers in the order you think they should be in.

1 Spray in short bursts

2 Leave the room

3 Shake well

4 Wash hands

5 Shut windows and doors

6 Keep closed for 10 to 15 minutes

4.2

TRF
PAGE 44

Listen to the instructions in the Teacher's File.

4.3

Words 1–7 are on a can of fly and wasp spray.
Match the words with the meanings a–g below.

Words	Meanings
1 EXPOSE	a) can burst into flames
2 INHALE	b) to be glowing with heat
3 FLAMMABLE	c) to make a hole in something
4 CAUTION	d) to breathe in
5 PIERCE	e) to go over the limit
6 EXCEED	f) put near, lay open to (high temperatures)
7 INCANDESCENT	g) take care; beware

4.4

Read this list of warnings from a fly spray can. Say what could
happen if you do not take care of each warning.

A Cover food before spraying

B Highly flammable

C Do not inhale

D Do not spray on a naked flame

E Keep out of the reach of children

F Extremely dangerous to fish

G Do not expose to temperatures that exceed 50°C

H Do not pierce the container

DAVIS AND TRAVERS VETERINARY SURGEONS

MA, VetMB, MRCVS and Associates
4, Hill Crescent, Senford,
Hen, HY5 7FQ
Tel: 01978 12345
or Fax: 01978 54321

MEMO

Robin

Thank you for agreeing to help us out at such short notice, yet again!
As promised, here are a few notes.

Please make answering the phone a priority. As before, customers can
bring their pets without an appointment at any time between half past four
and six o'clock. Otherwise they <u>must</u> be booked in. If you have any
problems ask Jane to help you.

If a farmer rings, you may need to get hold of Bob Davis. The trouble is,
he is not usually in the surgery. The most important thing is to make sure
you get the customer's name and phone number and a rough idea of
what the problem is. Then if Bob Davis is out, tell the customer you
will ring back. If Bob is not in surgery ring 09143 264. That will get him
wherever he is.

Would you take everyone a mug of coffee at around eleven o'clock,
with some biscuits (biscuits in the tin on the top shelf), and cups of
tea at about four.

If you have any spare time, I would be grateful if you could do some
filing for me. There's a pile on my desk!

By the way, open the post and if the results for the Winthrop's bull have
arrived let them know. Don't contact Winthrop himself, get his Farm
Manager, John Simms. The number is in their file.

Thanks for everything. I hope to be let out after the X-rays, so should be
back tomorrow.

Sue

priority – something that has to be done first

4.5

Read the letter opposite, then answer the questions below.

1 What part of the job is the most important?

2 If a customer wants to bring a pet to the vet in the morning, what must Robin do?

3 What must Robin be sure to do if a farmer rings with a problem?

4 How is Robin to get hold of Bob Davis if he is not in surgery?

5 *a)* Who must Robin phone if the results about the bull have arrived?
   b) How is Robin to find the phone number?

6 What must Robin do at about eleven and four o'clock?

7 What should Robin do if there are any problems?

8 Write down the words that tell you that Robin has helped out before.

9 What should Robin do if there is any spare time?

10 Where do you think Sue has gone for the day?

SEE ALSO
PAGES 115–116

There are two filing activities on pages 115 and 116 of this book.

4.6
SKILLS
PAGE 123

When about to leave school, Robin writes to Sue Jenkins to see if there is a chance of a job with the vets. Write this letter, using your own address and the information on page 34.

See pages 122 and 123 if you need help.

4.7

Read the passage that follows.

The buzzer sounded long and hard, it startled her even though
she knew to expect it. She splayed her book on the carpet so as
not to lose her place and went across the hall to her daughter's
bedroom. The girl was crouched on the bed, her face turned
5 towards the door in panic.

"Mum, another one," she said and pointed to her hand
pressed down hard on the pillow.

"Take it easy. Relax." Her mother hurried out of the bedroom
and came back with an empty pint glass from the kitchen.

10 "How can I relax with a thing like that in the bed? It might
breed, might be laying eggs."

"Wait."

"Dad uses a bar of soap. Don't let it get away." The girl's face
was anxious and much whiter than usual. She was wearing pyjama
15 bottoms and a football shirt of red and white hoops. "I hate them –
I hate them." Her voice was shaking. Her mother approached the
pillow with the pint glass inverted.

"Easy now – lift your hand."

The girl plucked her hand away. The black speck vanished – it
20 was there, then suddenly it wasn't – before the glass could be
slammed down. The girl screamed.

"It's jumped."

"Blast."

The girl held her hair back from her face, peering down at the
25 surface of the sheet.

"It's gone – it's got away."

"Aw no ..."

"Oh I hate them, I really hate them." The girl's voice was on the edge of tears. She was shuddering. "They make me feel so ... dirty." Her mother bent over and stared closely at the surface of
30 the white sheet, pulling it towards her a little to flatten a wrinkle.

"Don't move," she whispered. The girl gave a little gasp.

"Where? Where is it?"

Her mother raised the glass and quickly pressed it down onto the sheet.

35 "Gotcha."

The girl bent over and looked inside. She pulled up her lip in distaste when she saw the black speck.

"Eucchh." It jumped again and she squealed even though it was inside the glass. "I'm never going to let that cat in here again.
40 I hate it."

From *In Bed*, a short story by Bernard MacLaverty

4.8

Answer the questions below.

1 *a)* What was the girl frightened of?
   b) Make a list of the details from the text that tell you what it was.

2 Write down three words or phrases that let you know that the girl was frightened.

3 Has this happened to the girl before? How do you know?

4 What are some of the things that might happen next?

5 How would you feel if you were the person in the story? Are there any things you are frightened of?

4.9

Describe an insect or other animal that you are frightened of. Give as much detail as you can so that the reader can understand why it frightens you. You might want to describe:

- what it looks like
- the way it moves
- the sound it makes
- how it feels if you touch it.

4.10

In the passage below, Jonathan Raban has just rented a house in Guntersville, in America. Read the passage.

It took me a while to spot the ants. Unpacking my bag in the bathroom, I thought I saw the brown shagpile carpet ripple like a cornfield in a wind. Looking closer, I saw a colony of ants the size of wasps out on some kind of jungle exercise in the woolly
5 undergrowth. When I flushed the lavatory, a hundred or so ant-marines tumbled into the toilet bowl from their positions under the rim.

I drove the car back into town, a mile away, and consulted my new friend William, the pharmacist.
10 'They black ants? Or are they a kind of reddy-brown?'
'Black – I think.'
'I *hope* it's black ants you got out there. If they're a *brown* ant, it could be, you got *fire ants* on your place. Then you got problems.' He was hunting round among his poisons.
15 'Friend of mine, he had fire ants once, he just went out into his back yard one morning, end of the day, his daughter came home, found him lying there *dayud*. Fire ants. Yes – he was killed by fire ants,' he said ...

As he spoke, my ants started changing colour rapidly from
20 black to brown.

'But if they're inside your house, they'll most likely be black ants. I hope so anyway; I wouldn't like to think of you with fire ants in your house. How big you say they are?'

I found it hard to control the trembling of my forefinger
25 and thumb.

William nodded and smiled; he looked pleased by what I'd shown him.

'Oh yes, we do get them real big around here –'

Before I left the drugstore with two bottles of sweet antbane, he
30 asked me about brown recluse spiders. They were worse than fire ants; far worse. There was probably a brown recluse somewhere out at my place; most people had them without knowing.

Slightly adapted from *Hunting Mister Heartbreak* by Jonathan Raban

shagpile carpet – carpet where the tufts are long
marine – a soldier on duty in a ship
pharmacist – chemist

4.11

Answer the questions below.

1 Jonathan Raban describes the ants as being on a jungle exercise (line 4). Why is this a good description?

2 Why do you think that in line 6 Jonathan Raban describes some of the ants as 'ant-marines'?

3 *a)* What are the two sorts of ants that could be in the house?
b) How can you tell them apart?
c) Why is it important to know which sort are in the house?

4 Jonathan Raban says: 'As he spoke my ants started changing colour ...'
a) What does he mean by this?   *b)* Why did he say this?

5 What do you think the word 'dayud' means (line 17)?

6 What do you think that the sweet antbane is for (line 29)?

7 When William speaks, he misses out some words that would normally be present in a proper sentence. Write down the words that are missing from his speech in lines (12–14), (15–18) and in the last sentence of line 23.

8 What things do you think might happen next?

9 How would you feel if you were Jonathan Raban? What would you do next?

4.12

OPTIONS

1 Continue the story. Describe what happens when you get back home and how you feel. Imagine you are the person in the story and use your own way of writing.

2 Imagine you have interviewed Jonathan Raban about his experiences. Write your account for a local newspaper.

See pages 13 and 28 if you need ideas.

SEE ALSO

PAGES 13, 28

4.13

Work in groups of three or four.

1 Pick one of the statements below to discuss.

2 Pick someone in your group to jot down the ideas you have.

3 In your group work out reasons either FOR or AGAINST the statement.

4 Pick someone in your group to tell the rest of the class what you have discussed.

5 Ask the group for their ideas.

A We should not kill insects. Wasps, flies and fleas have as much right to life as us.

B We should not spend money on feeding and looking after animals. That money should be used to feed people who have not enough food.

C Fishing should be banned; it's cruel.

D We care more about animals than old people.

E Birds should be left in the wild, not caged as pets.

F Animals should not be used for experiments.

4.14

TRF
PAGE 11

SEE ALSO
PAGES 13, 28

OPTIONS

1 Use the information from the discussion to give a talk either FOR or AGAINST one of the statements.

2 Your local paper is running a PET SPOT. Readers give details about their pets, describe the tricks they can do, etc. Write about your pet for the local paper.

4.15 **Read the poem below. Only part of it is printed here.**

Chase me, follow me round the room, knock over
Chairs and tables, bruise knees, spill books. High
I am then. If you climb up to me I go
Down. I have ways of detecting your least
Movements. I have radar you did not
Invent. You are afraid of me, I can ...

4.16 **Answer the question below.**

What is the 'I' in the poem? Why do you think this?

4.17 **Now turn over and read the whole poem on the next page.**

Chase me, follow me round the room, knock over
Chairs and tables, bruise knees, spill books. High
I am then. If you climb up to me I go
Down. I have ways of detecting your least
5 Movements. I have radar you did not
Invent. You are afraid of me, I can
Sting hard. Ah but watch me bask in
The, to you, unbearable sun. I sport with it, am
Its jester and also its herald. Fetch a
10 Fly whisk. I scorn such. You must invent stings
For yourselves or else leave alone, small, flying,
Buzzing tiger who have made a jungle out of the room
    you thought safe,
Secure from all hurts and prying.

Elizabeth Jennings

jester – joker, someone who plays tricks
herald – something or someone that comes before
    or tells you that something is on the way
secure – safe
prying – peeping into private places

4.18

Answer the questions below.

1 Have you changed your mind about what kind of insect or
   animal the 'I' is in the poem? Which details made you change
   your mind?

2 The insect in the poem is described as a tiger.
   a) In what ways is the insect like a tiger?
   b) Which three words describe the insect but
       could not be used to describe a tiger?

3 The insect says it has 'made a jungle out of the room'.
   In what ways has it done this?

4 The insect in the poem says it is safe. In your own words
   list the reasons why it thinks it is safe.

5 Do you like this poem? Say why.

Take the weather with you

Around Britain Met office report for 24 hours to 5 p.m. yesterday

	Sun hrs	Rain in	Temp (°C) H	L	Weather (day)
Manchester	3.3	0.06	15	9	Rain a.m.
Margate	2.0	–	15	9	Bright a.m.
Minehead	1.6	–	16	11	Cloudy
Morecambe	7.5	–	14	11	Sunny
Newcastle	7.0	0.08	13	9	Sunny
Oxford	1.7	0.05	13	7	Drizzle p.m.

hrs: hours; in: inches; Temp: temperature; H: high; L: low.

met office – the weather office
p.m. – afternoon, that is, mid-day to midnight
a.m. – morning, that is, midnight to mid-day

5.1

Look at the weather chart above. Then answer the questions.

1 Where did the details above come from?

2 *a)* Which place had the most sunshine?
  b) How many hours of sunshine did it have?

3 What was the weather like in Manchester in the morning?

4 Which town had the coldest weather?

5 Read the details for Oxford. Now put the information into a full sentence. (Do not use shortened words.)

5.2

Listen to the report in the Teacher's File.

TRF
PAGE 51

The great

COVER-UP

Sun damage can be avoided. Experts believe that in four out of every five cases skin cancer is a preventable disease. To look after your skin, the golden rules are:

head for the shade
around midday

In the hours around midday the sun is at its highest in the sky. The rays of the sun do not have so far to travel and it does not take so long to burn.

take care not to burn

Sunburn is not just painful. Even if the burnt skin gets better quickly, some permanent damage may remain. Sunburn leads to greater risk of skin cancer in later life.

cover up

Clothing is the best sunscreen. A loose fit will help to keep you cool. Pick a wide-brimmed hat. It will help to shade your nose and ears, the most common places for skin cancer. Don't forget your sunglasses – pick ones labelled BS2724: 1987 for good protection.

use a high-factor sunscreen

Choose a sunscreen with SPF 15 or above. Try not to depend on sunscreen to protect your skin. You should still try not to spend too much time in the sun. When you use sunscreen, put it on thickly and keep adding more during the day.

preventable – can be avoided

permanent – lasting

SPF number – tells you how much protection from the sun you can get. The SPF number is on the front of a bottle of sun cream

5.3

Read the leaflet opposite. Then answer the questions.

1 What disease do you risk getting if you get burnt by the sun?

2 Write down the 'four golden rules' for looking after your skin.

3 Why might you get more burnt by the sun at midday?

4 Why do you need a wide-brimmed hat when you are in the sun?

5 What sort of sunglasses should you use?

6 What SPF number should you look for on a sunscreen?

7 Write down the two words in the text that mean 'something that need not happen'.

5.4

SKILLS

PAGES 120–121

OPTIONS

1 Mrs Kent is very upset because her six-year-old daughter sat for two hours in the sun on a hot summer's day. She was wearing a short-sleeved summer dress and no hat and she was not in the shade. It was the Felton Primary School Sports Day Practice.

   Write the letter of complaint Mrs Kent sends to the Headteacher, Mr L. Johns. The address of the school is Felton, Berkshire FG8 7LG. Use your own address. See pages 120 and 121 if you need help.

SEE ALSO

PAGE 20

TRF

PAGES 52–55

2 Rewrite and design the leaflet opposite to make it suitable for children of 6–8 years old. There may be some details you do not think they will need. Use pictures to help the children remember what is important. (You do not need to draw pictures, just show where they would go and what they would be about.) For example, see page 20 in this book and 52–55 in the TRF.

Read the play below.

The action takes place late at night. Samuel and Maxine are in bed, in their flat. The date is October 15th, 1987, the night when hurricane force winds started to sweep across southern England. The play was written for radio and is spoken to a reggae beat.

wa – what or what's
dat – that
dem – them
mek – make

Hurricane Dub

The sound of wind builds. Music. Then there is a big crash, the sound of a tree falling on a car.

SAMUEL: Wa dat?
MAXINE: Me nuh know.
SAMUEL: Wa dat?
MAXINE: Me nuh know.
5   SAMUEL: Wa dat?
MAXINE: Me nuh know, me nuh know, me nuh know. Check it out. Check it out.
SAMUEL: Sound like a car get damage. Sound like a car crash.
MAXINE: Mek a dash and see if it's your G.T.
10   SAMUEL: Oh Lord, not me, not my G.T.
      (Going off.) Mek me see. Mek me see.
MAXINE: What do you see?
SAMUEL: It's not my G.T., but the Ford next door
      has been hit by a tree.
15   MAXINE: Flying trees!
SAMUEL: *(Getting back into bed.)* It's gettin' bad out there.
      I hope nothing happens to my G.T.
MAXINE: Come lie down. We can't sleep but let's rest.
      De emergency services will do dem best.
20   SAMUEL: I suppose you're right, but God what a night.
      In de morning there will be a dreadful sight.

Music. A short burst of drumbeat.

MAXINE: Where yu goin' now? Why can't yu be humble?
SAMUEL: I jus' a listen to de news. Listen, I beg yu stop grumble.

25   *Crackle as he turns on the radio. Some interference.*
            Then Big Ben strikes the hour.

BBC NEWSREADER: Dis is de news from the BBC
                We transmit round the world and locally
                Every hour on the hour with a weather forecast.
30   And right now in the South of England, breeze blowing fast.
                Shipping people beware and drivers drive with care
                And we suggest that if you're out at sea, you should be here.
                Party people and burglars better go home.
                The disabled and the elderly should use the telephone.
                It's wicked and it's wild in the London region.

                                                    Benjamin Zephaniah

5.6

Answer these questions.

1 Read lines 8–14 again. Then write down all the words that rhyme.

2 Re-read lines 1–7. Clap out the rhythm. Then read these lines out loud trying to keep the reggae rhythm.

3 How will the newsreader's voice sound different to Samuel's and Maxine's voices?

4 What words make the BBC broadcast sound real?

5 What details make the BBC weather forecast real and not so real?

6 In this part of the play what is Samuel most worried about?

7 Samuel says, 'In de morning there will be a dreadful sight.' What sort of sight might they see when they look out of the window?

8 Now read the play out loud, trying to get the beat and rhythm as well as the meaning.

9 You could make a tape of this, using the sound effects suggested in the script.

a

b

Winter

When icicles hang by the wall,
 And Dick the shepherd blows his nail,
And Tom bears logs into the hall,
 And milk comes frozen in the pail;
5 When blood is nipped, and ways be foul,
Then nightly sings the staring owl.
Tu-wit, Tu-who! A merry note,
While greasy Joan doth keel the pot.

c

When all aloud the wind doth blow,
10 And coughing drowns the parson's saw,
And birds sit brooding in the snow,
  And Marian's nose looks red and raw,
When roasted crabs hiss in the bowl,
Then nightly sings the staring owl,
15 Tu-wit, Tu-who! a merry note,
While greasy Joan doth keel the pot.

William Shakespeare

e

d

blows his nail – to wait
pail – bucket
foul – muddy
keel the pot – to stir so that the food in the pot does not boil over
drowns – here, makes so much noise that you cannot hear
saw – here, a sermon or talk
crabs – small, sour apples called crab apples

5.7 Read the poem on page 48, then answer the questions.

1 Look at pictures **a** to **i** carefully. Match each picture with a line from the poem, for example, **d** = line 12.

2 What details in the poem are not so likely to happen any more? Say what we have in their place.

3 What details in the poem make you remember how cold winter is?

4 Make a list of some of the details that remind you of winter now.

5 Write down one thing you like or dislike about winter. Try to describe it so that the person reading it will feel what it is like. Now add four more things you like or dislike and describe these. Present your work on one side of paper and illustrate it.

Ready for work

SL

Simon Langley Distributors
OFFICE JUNIOR

**We have a vacancy for an office junior.
Aged 16–17, you must be of smart
appearance and willing to learn.
Good prospects for advancement.**

Apply for an application form to:
Mrs D. Thomas,
Simon Langley Distributors
Langley House,
26–28 Station Road,
Newcastle upon Tyne NE6 9DV

Include an SAE
Closing date Friday 28th June 1996

vacancy – a job is available
prospects – chances, opportunities
advancement – getting a better job
SAE – **S**tamped and **A**ddressed **E**nvelope; this means you
have to send a stamped envelope with your address on it,
so that it does not cost the people you are writing to
anything to send you a reply

6.1 Read the advertisement opposite, then answer the questions.

1 What company is offering the job?

2 What is the job that is being advertised?

3 How old do you have to be for the job?

4 What kind of person does the company want?

5 What do you have to do if you want to apply for the job?

6 By what date must all application forms be filled in and
sent to the company?

6.2

PAGES 125–126

TRF
PAGES 59–65

OPTIONS

1 Write to ask for an application form for the job advertised on
the opposite page. (See page 125 if you need help.) Use your
own address.
  Draw and address the two envelopes. (See page 126.)

2 The advertisement wanted people of smart appearance.
Make a list of some of the things someone could do to
make themselves look smart.

Simon Langley

Please use Block Letters

APPLICATION FOR THE POST OF

SURNAME   **FORENAMES IN FULL**

ADDRESS

POSTCODE

TEL NO   **AGE**   **D.O.B.**   **NEXT OF KIN**

EXAMINATIONS PASSED – *(indicate if you are waiting for any results)*

School   Date   Subject   Grade   Exam (GCSE, GNVQ, etc.)

QUALIFICATIONS GAINED THROUGH EMPLOYMENT – *(include dates)*

DETAILS OF PREVIOUS EMPLOYMENT

Dates of employment   Employer's name & address   Duties

ACTIVITIES AND INTERESTS e.g. sports, hobbies, social.

PLEASE GIVE YOUR REASONS FOR APPLYING FOR THIS JOB

Give names and addresses of two referees. Include one from your last employer, or if you are a school leaver, from your headteacher. Do not include relatives.

NAME   **NAME**

ADDRESS   **ADDRESS**

Return to: Personnel, Simon Langley, Langley House, 26–28 Station Road, Newcastle upon Tyne, NE6 9DV

block letters – capital letters

post – job

surname – last name, e.g. Smith is the surname of John Smith

Tel – telephone

No – number

D.O.B. – date of birth, the day you were born

next of kin – your nearest relative. If you are not married, your mother or father or sister may be your next of kin. If you are married, your husband or wife is your next of kin

referee – in this case, someone who will give you a reference

6.3

TRF

PAGE 59

Read the form opposite, then answer the questions below.

1 Write out your details for the first part of the form (from 'surname' to 'next of kin'). There is a blank copy of the form in the Teacher's File.

2 Work out what you could put under the heading 'ACTIVITIES AND INTERESTS'. Give details of any achievements or positions you have held. Then write out a neat copy of the information.

6.4

1 I want some money

2 I know this is a good firm to work for

3 I like the uniform

4 I like meeting people

5 I want to learn more

6 My mate works here

7 The job offers me the opportunity of learning a skill or trade

8 It will give me experience

9 My Mum/Dad/Nan says I have to get a job

10 I am interested in (animals, engineering, young children, etc.)

11 The pay is good.

Look at the reasons listed above, for why people want a job. Which reasons would be good to put on a form for a job as:

a) an office helper

b) a motor mechanic

c) a trainee hairdresser

d) a hospital porter.

BRENTFORD FIBRES LTD

MEMO

To: All staff

NEW SECURITY ARRANGEMENTS

As you all know, during the past few years there have been some serious breaches of security within the offices and some distressing incidents in the car parks. For these reasons the following measures have been introduced.

1. IDENTITY TAGS

From February 1st all personnel will wear Brentford identity tags at all times whilst at work. For this purpose a photographer will be in the buildings on January 14th and 15th from 9.30 a.m. to 12.30 p.m. and from 2 p.m. to 4 p.m. If you know you are going to be away on those dates, please inform your Line Manager who will make other arrangements.

2. NEW SECURITY LOCKS

A new combination locks security system will be installed over the weekend of January 30th and 31st. These will be fitted to two main entrances. The code will be given to you at your meetings on Monday February 1st. I would like to stress here, **do not give this number to anyone other than a member of the firm**.

3. SECURITY ARRANGEMENTS FOR VISITORS

Visitors will be required to sign a visitors' register and wear a visitor's identity tag. If you are expecting any visitors, inform reception with as much detail as possible, e.g. name, firm, job description, purpose of visit, times of arrival and departure. When the full tagging system is in place, from February 1st, inform internal security immediately if you see anyone not displaying an identity tag.

4. CAR PARK ARRANGEMENTS

From February 1st all cars must display identity discs. These will be made at the same time as the identity tags. Lighting will be installed in the car park and security personnel employed from 7 a.m. to 8.30 p.m. on all weekdays. If you know you will be working later, you MUST notify the security office, so that arrangements can be made for security personnel to stay on.

These security arrangements are for everyone's benefit.

Stephanie Chang

Stephanie Chang
Operations Manager

breach – break. If there has been a **breach in security** it perhaps means that someone has got into the buildings or that there has been a leak of information

distressing – upsetting

incident – something out of the ordinary that has happened

personnel – people working with a firm

identity tag – badge or disc you'd wear to let people know who you are

installed – put in; fitted

departure – when something or someone goes away from a place

to display – to show, to put in a place so that people can see

6.5

Read the memo opposite. It has been sent to every employee in the firm where you work. Then answer the questions below.

1 Why have new security arrangements been introduced?

2 From what date will employees be expected to wear identity tags?

3 On what dates is the photographer visiting the firm?

4 What should you do if you are away on the dates that the photographer is visiting?

5 Where are the new security locks to be fitted?

6 When will you know the code for the new security locks?

7 What must you be sure not to do when you know the code?

8 When will visitors start to wear identity tags?

9 What other arrangements have been made for visitors?

10 What should you do if you see someone without an identity tag after February 1st?

11 Between what hours will there be security personnel in the firm's car park?

12 What should you do if you want to work later?

13 Who has sent this memorandum?

6.6

Listen to the talk in the Teacher's File.

TRF

PAGES 66–68

THE DO'S AND DONT'S
of what to wear for a job interview

DO wear something smart and simple. There's no need to buy new clothes or wear anything very expensive, as long as you look tidy and show you have made an effort.

DON'T wear anything too bright. It's usually best to stick to neutral colours, with black, blue and grey being the best options. But it depends on the colour of your eyes and hair, plus the tone of your skin. A white shirt or blouse can make one person look timid while another will look outgoing and full of energy.

DO be careful about jewellery, perfume and make-up. Cut down on anything that might not fit in with the firm.

DON'T leave it to the last minute to plan what you are going to wear. Try on your outfit a few days before to make sure it is in good order.

DO sew on any missing buttons and repair hems that are coming down. Polish your shoes the night before.

DON'T risk getting a ladder in your tights or stockings. Take a spare pair with you just in case.

DO remember, clothes often speak louder than words.

Most interviews are decided in the first 30 seconds, according to the big firms that specialise in finding jobs.

neutral colours – colours that are not too bright
clothes speak louder than words – clothes say more about what
  you are like than what you tell someone about yourself

6.7

Read the article opposite, then answer the questions.

1 Why do you think it might be a good idea to try on your outfit
  a few days before the interview?

2 What are the best colours to wear for an interview?

3 What can someone who wears tights do to make sure they
  do not go to the interview with a ladder?

4 *a)* 'Clothes often speak louder than words.' What does this mean?
  b) Do you agree? Say why.

5 *a)* How long does it take most interviewers to make up their
    mind about whether someone is suitable for a job?
  b) Why do you think this is?

6.8
SKILLS
PAGE 124

**Pick one of the jobs from the advertisement below. Imagine you have
filled in an application form for the job. Write the letter you could
send with the application form. See page 125 if you need help.**

CHEGLEYS SUPER STORES

12, Hillcourt Road, Stredley
Due to expansion, we have part-time and
full-time vacancies in the following areas.

**CHECKOUT
SNACK BAR
BAKERY
SHELF STACKING
HARDWARE
SERVICE STATION
OFFICE
WAREHOUSE**

Phone Jan Betts, 01876 3942, for an application form.

Read the extract below.

It was hot in the little bus and I was on the wrong side where the July sun beat on the windows. I shifted uncomfortably inside my best suit and eased a finger inside the tight white collar. It was a foolish outfit for this weather, but I was going for an interview and
5 I had to make a good impression.

It hadn't seemed true when the letter came from Darrowby in the Yorkshire Dales. Mr Farnon, Veterinary Surgeon, would like to see me on the Friday afternoon; I was to come to tea and if we got on with each other, I could stay on to be his assistant.
10 The driver crashed his gears again as we went into another steep bend. We had been climbing now for the last fifteen miles. I had seen the fences and hedges give way to dry stone walls. The walls were everywhere, miles of them.

Soon the bus was clattering along a narrow street which opened
15 on to a square where we stopped. Above the window of a grocer shop I read 'Darrowby Co-op'. We had arrived.

Trengate was a quiet street leading off the square. Now that I was here, right on the doorstep, I felt breathless, as though I had been running. If I got the job, this would be where I would find
20 out about myself. There were many things to prove.

I rang the doorbell and instantly the afternoon peace was shattered by a distant barking, like a wolf pack in full cry. The upper half of the door was of glass and, as I peered through, a river of dogs poured round the corner of a long passage and
25 dashed itself with frenzied yells against the door. I stepped back and watched as the dogs appeared, sometimes two at a time, at the top of their leap, eyes glaring, jaws slavering.

I was thinking of ringing the bell again when I saw a large woman at the end of the passage. She rapped out a single word
30 and the noise stopped as if by magic. When she opened the door the pack was slinking round her feet, showing the whites of their eyes and wagging their tucked in tails.

"Good afternoon," I said with my best smile. "My name is Herriot. Mr Farnon is expecting me."

35 "Mr Herriot?" she said thoughtfully. "Surgery is from six o'clock to seven. If you want to bring a dog in, that would be your best time."

"No, no," I said, hanging on to my smile. "I'm applying for the position of assistant. Mr Farnon said to come in time for tea."

40 "Assistant? Well now, that's nice." The lines in her face softened a little. "I'm Mrs Hall. I keep house for Mr Farnon. He never said anything to me about you. He's gone to visit his mother. I don't know when he'll be back. Never mind. Come in and have a cup of tea."

Adapted from *If Only They Could Talk* by James Herriot

veterinary surgeon – a doctor for animals
jaws slavering – spit and foam coming from the mouth

6.10

Answer these questions.

1 What job is James Herriot hoping to get?

2 Why did James Herriot feel that it was important to wear a suit?

3 On lines 19 and 20 James Herriot says 'I would find out about myself' and 'There were many things to prove.'
a) What do you think he might mean by these two statements?
b) Write down two things that he might 'have to prove'.

4 Why does Mrs Hall think James Herriot has called at the house? (lines 35 to 37?)

5 Read lines 40 to 44 again.
a) Explain in your own words why James Herriot might be surprised by what Mrs Hall tells him.
b) How do you think he would feel about this?
c) What do you think might have happened?

6 The extract came from a book called *If Only They Could Talk*.
a) What do you think 'they' stands for?
b) Why do you think that James Herriot wished that 'they' could talk?

7

Money, money, money

7.1

John England owes a friend some money. Read the details about the cheque he fills in.

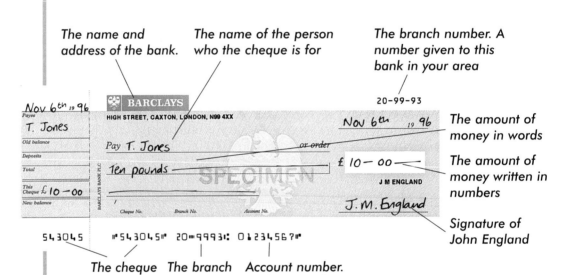

The name and address of the bank.

The name of the person who the cheque is for

The branch number. A number given to this bank in your area

The amount of money in words

The amount of money written in numbers

Signature of John England

The cheque number

The branch number

Account number. Each person has their own number

7.2

Answer the questions below.

1 Which bank does John England belong to?

2 How much money is he paying out to his friend?

3 What is the name of the friend who is getting the money?

4 What is John England's account number?

5 Which branch is John's bank and what is the number?

6 What will be the number of the next cheque that John writes?

7.3

Read how to fill in a cheque.

line, so no other name can be added

number written close to edge

Pay Gill Smith ——————— or order

Ten pounds, 99p only ————

£ 10 — 99 ——

J M ENGLAND

BARCLAYS BANK PLC

SPECIMEN

7.4

Read the list of instructions below. Say what could happen if you do not follow each of the instructions.

> **permanent ink** – ink that does not come off, e.g. ballpoint
> **an alteration** – a change

1 If your cheque book is lost or stolen let the bank know at once.
2 Write your cheque in permanent ink.
3 Sign your name against any alterations.
4 Write the amount in numbers, as close to the pound sign as possible.
5 Put a line between the pounds and pence, not a dot, e.g. £10–99

7.5

Fill in the sample cheques in the Teacher's File.

TRF
PAGE 70

 **Midlands Electricity plc**

Mrs L F Smith
42 Elm Road
Selford
Shrewsbury
SH4 8PL

26th June 1996

Dear Mrs Smith

CUSTOMER REFERENCE NUMBER 8695/82530/91
AMOUNT DUE £92.53

Our records show that this bill remains unpaid. Unless you
have paid in the last few days, please pay now. If you are
unable to pay, please call our advice line on

01905 613191

We will help you choose a way to pay that is best for you.

Please ring us now.

If you do not pay or contact us, we have the right to cut off
your supply. Should we need to take action you will have to
pay extra costs.

So if you cannot pay, please ring us now.

Yours sincerely,
Mrs Joan Sands,
Payments Manager

Enquiries   **MEB, BLACKPOLE ROAD, WORCESTER, WR4 9TB**
to: **(8.00am - 6.00pm Mon to Fri, 9.00am - 1.00pm Sat)**

Registered Office: Mucklow Hill, Halesowen, West Midlands, B62 8BP Registered in England and Wales: No. 2366928.

plc – public limited company

7.6

Read the letter on page 62, then answer the questions.

1 What is this letter about?

2 What is Mrs Smith's reference number?

3 How much money does Mrs Smith owe?

4 If she cannot pay the bill, what should she do?

5 What phone number should she call?

6 If Mrs Smith phones to say that she cannot pay, how can the MEB help her?

7 What might happen if Mrs Smith does not pay the bill and she does not write to or phone the MEB?

7.7

SEE ALSO
PAGE 56

OPTIONS

1 Make a chart of **Top Tips** or a **Do and Don't** chart for a family needing to save money. (See page 56 for an example.)

2 Mr Evans has an electricity bill for £69.40. It is due to be paid in ten days' time on March 17th. Mr Evans cannot pay by this date, but he will have the money on April 2nd.

   Write the letter he could send to the MEB to ask them if they will allow him to pay on this date. His customer number is 6542/609871/23. Use your own address.

SKILLS
PAGE 119

7.8

TRF
PAGE 74

Listen to the talk in the Teacher's File.

Now you only pay for the time you talk. Precisely.

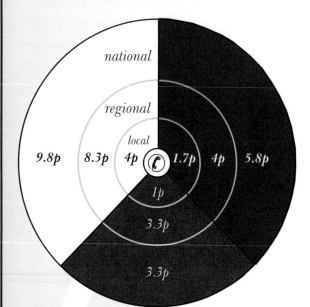

national over 35 miles
regional up to 35 miles
local within your local call area.

Price per minute for a UK call
5p minimum charge for all calls.
Prices include VAT. Different
prices apply to BT Chargecard
calls and calls made from payphones.

℡ **You**
The caller

○ **Daytime**
Mon to Fri 8 a.m.–6 p.m.

● **Evenings & night-time**
Mon to Fri before 8 a.m. & after 6 p.m.

● **Weekend**
Midnight Fri to Midnight Sun

British Telecommunications plc
Registered office:
81 Newgate Street, London EC1A 7AJ

per – each
minimum charge – the smallest amount of money
VAT – **V**alue **A**dded **T**ax; a tax that is sometimes
   added to a bill
BT – **B**ritish **T**elecom
a.m. – the morning: after midnight and up to 12 o'clock lunch time
p.m. – after 12 o'clock lunch time and up to midnight
Mon to Fri – **Mon**day to **Fri**day

7.9

Look at the details on page 64, then answer the questions.

1 What colour on the chart tells you the cost of phone
   calls in the daytime?

2 When is the cheapest time to make a phone call?

3 If you make a phone call at 6.30 p.m. on a Wednesday,
   which colour on the chart should you look at to check
   the cost of your call?

4 Look at the meanings of the words national, regional and local.
   a) If you phone a friend who lives 40 miles away, which of
      the words above describes your phone call?
   b) When is a phone call local?

5 There are three rings in the chart – outside,
   in-between and inside.
   a) Which ring tells you the cost of phone calls to
      places over 35 miles away?
   b) Which ring tells you the cost of local calls?

6 *a)* You phone a friend at the weekend who lives in the
      same town as you. You talk for ten minutes. How much
      would it cost?
   b) You phone the same friend on Monday morning at
      10.00 a.m. Again you talk for ten minutes. How much
      would this phone call cost?
   c) You phone an aunt that evening who lives 50 miles away.
      You talk for one minute. How much will that phone call cost?

7 *a)* Explain in your own words what the sentence below means:
      '5p minimum charge for all calls.'
   b) You ring a friend at the weekend who lives a mile from you.
      You talk for four minutes. How much would it cost?

Peter Craig

Balcarres Road, Preston, PR2 2FD

Miss L James
4 Church Road
Sittingbourne
Kent
ME10 8GF
429588473   SB

Dear Miss James

It gives me great pleasure to inform you that you have been chosen to receive a Special Cash Award. A total of £1,000,000 has been allocated by our computer and you have been selected to receive a share of the payout.

A cash amount has already been reserved for you and, as soon as we receive your authorisation, we will mail out a cheque in your name. It could be anything from £1 up to £10, £100, £1,000, £10,000 or even £100,000.

Waiting for the catch? Well, there isn't one. We just thought we'd like to celebrate the launch of the new Peter Craig Catalogue. All you need to do is return the claim form enclosed in the envelope provided (even the postage is free).

However, please note: we are unable to release your cheque unless we receive your claim within the next 14 days. After this time, your cash award will, unfortunately, have to be forfeited and cannot be re-offered at a later date – so please hurry.

Along with your cheque, we would also like to send you a complimentary copy of our new catalogue. Naturally, I hope you will like it and want to order something. Especially as I have enclosed an introductory 20% discount voucher for you to use.

May I offer you my sincere congratulations on your Cash Award and I look forward to dispatching your cheque.

Yours sincerely

Ruth Porter

General Manager

allocated – placed on one side for you
reserved – set aside for you
authorise – to give permission
forfeit – give up
introductory – here, first time
discount – money is taken off

7.10

Read the letter opposite and then answer the questions.

1 What company sent this letter?

2 Why have they sent the letter?

3 What is the main way that the company have tried to persuade people to take up the offer?

4 What words and phrases make you feel that you have been picked out?

5 What words and phrases in the letter might make you feel as if you are being offered something very special?

6 List the ways the company have used to get you to take up their offer. Use your own words as much as possible.

7 What do you have to do if you want to take up this offer?

8 On the real letter, all the sentences of a whole paragraph had been underlined. Which paragraph do you think it was? Say why.

9 Two other parts (both about 2–3 centimetres long) were underlined. What do you think they were? Why?

TRF
PAGE 69

Details of which parts were underlined can be found in the Teacher's File.

7.11

Someone wants to buy a cassette player. Write down some of the places they could buy it from, e.g. a car-boot sale, a catalogue, a free advertisement page in a newspaper, etc. Write down the **'fors'** and **'againsts'** of buying at each place.

A

I don't care too much for money
For money can't buy me love
Can't buy me love
Everybody tells me so ...

From *Can't buy me love*, a Beatles song

B

Annual income twenty pounds, annual expenditure
nineteen (pounds) nineteen (shillings) and six (pence),
result happiness.

Annual income twenty pounds, annual expenditure
twenty pounds, no (shillings) and six (pence), result misery.

From *David Copperfield* by Charles Dickens; said by Mr Micawber

C

The best things in life are free

From 1927 song by B. De Sylva and L. Brown

D

I want to be a millionaire

E

The love of money is the root of all evil

From Timothy, in *The Bible*

F

When lottery winners say their millions will not change the way
we live, most of us smile sourly ... So it is particularly delightful
to read that Alan Baker, who won £9 million, has gone back to
work after a month because he is so bored. And his wife has
gone back to her £125-a-week job.

Katharine Whitehorn in *The Observer*

annual – yearly
income – the money coming in
a shilling – a coin that was worth 12 old pence,
    or 5 new pence
expenditure – money spent
the root of all evil – the cause of all badness

7.12

Read A–F on the opposite page. Then, in a group, answer the questions below.

Extract A

1 Why is the singer not very interested in money?

2 How much do you agree with this? Say why you think this is true and not true.

Extract B

1 What makes Mr Micawber happy?

2 What makes Mr Micawber unhappy?

3 Explain in your own words what Mr Micawber is saying.

4 How much do you agree with Mr Micawber? Give reasons why you might agree and disagree.

Extract C

1 Make a list of 'best things' that are free.

2 Make a list of some 'best things' that are not free.

3 How much do you agree with the saying? Give reasons why you agree and disagree.

Extract D

1 Would you want to be a millionaire? Make a list of reasons why you would and would not.

Extract E

1 What does this saying mean?

2 Make a list of some of the ways that this is true and not true.

Extract F

1 What did Mr and Mrs Baker do when they won £9 million on the lottery?

2 What do you think you would do if you won a large sum of money on the lottery? Say why.

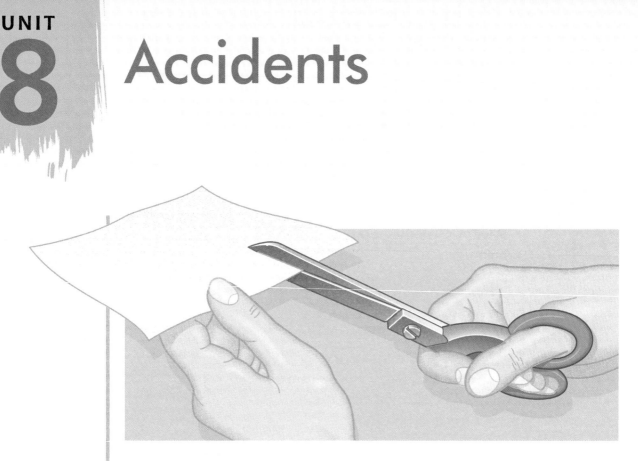

8.1

The instructions 1 to 6 below tell you how to treat a cut, but they are in the wrong order. Write down the numbers in the order you think they should be in.

1 Dry with a piece of gauze.

2 Wash hands before treating the wound.

3 Keep in place by putting on a dressing tape or a bandage.

4 Clean the wound under running water.

5 Wash your hands after treating the wound.

6 Cut a fresh piece of gauze to the size and shape needed.

Listen to the messages in the Teacher's File, and answer the questions.

8.2

TRF
PAGE 84

8.3

People insure their property so that they can replace it if it is lost or damaged. Look at the words below. They are often used on insurance forms.

> **insurance policy** – a legal agreement to pay sums of money if something is lost or damaged
>
> **premium** – a payment   **cover** – protect
>
> **valid** – will work
>
> **calendar month** – one of the months of the year such as 'April'
>
> **'certain'** – the word 'certain' sometimes comes in front of a list of things that may happen to your property, e.g. 'certain' fire. The word 'certain' here means that your property is not protected against ALL fire. For example, you would not be protected if you set fire to your own house on purpose
>
> **permanent residence** – a place where you live most of the time
>
> **maximum** – the biggest number
>
> **minimum** – the lowest number
>
> **vehicle** – a method of transport such as a car, bicycle, motorcycle, etc.

8.4

Read the passage below. In the passage Jon has phoned to ask about getting an insurance policy. Write down the missing words using one of the words from the box below.

premium	policy	insure	cover

Jon   Hello. I'd like to _ _ _ _ _ _ my bike.
Can I do that with you?

Ann   Yes. We have a _ _ _ _ _ _ which will _ _ _ _ _ bicycles.
How much do you need to insure your bike for?

Jon   Well, how much would it cost to insure my bike for a year?

Ann   That depends on how much your bike is worth. If you want to insure it for £100, then the _ _ _ _ _ _ _ would be £14. But I would need to know more about your bike.

8.5

Look at the information below. It gives details about how to insure your possessions.

INSURANCE

National Best Selling Policy

BEST VALUE FOR MONEY

PERSONAL POSSESSIONS INSURANCE

Away from home? Your personal possessions stand a very real chance of being stolen or destroyed. Can you afford to replace them? If not, then this is the policy for you. The cost is very small when compared to the total value involved. This scheme gives wider cover and offers probably the best value for money around, for 12 months cover. Cover is also available on a monthly policy (valid for one calendar month).

WHAT IS COVERED?

You receive £5000 of Insurance Cover i.e.

- £2500 cover for your personal possessions for certain fire, theft and water damage.
- £2500 cover for certain fire and theft for any landlord's/college's/school's property in your room(s).

WHERE ARE MY PERSONAL POSSESSIONS COVERED?

- At your college/school or permanent home address.
- When travelling between your home and term time residence at the beginning and end of each term.

CAN I INSURE MY PEDAL CYCLE?

Yes, and in fact many pedal cycles are stolen every year, so it is a wise move. You can insure your cycle for a minimum of £100 to a maximum of £500. Minimum premium £14 for a yearly policy, £1.40 for a monthly policy.

WHAT ABOUT ALL RISKS COVER FOR MY VALUABLES?

We recommend you take our All Risks Cover (Section D on the Proposal Form) to extend cover for your more valuable items such as cameras to protect against loss, damage and theft (except theft from vehicles), anywhere in the U.K.

INCLUDED IN YOUR POLICY FREE OF CHARGE

ILLEGAL USE OF CREDIT CARDS – up to £1000.

Plus PERSONAL ACCIDENT

You are covered for up to £1000 if you have an accident caused by the use of the insured items.

8.6 Answer the following questions. If you cannot remember the meanings of some of the words, turn back to page 71.

1 On this policy, what is the shortest time you can get cover for your personal possessions?

2 If you take out insurance for your personal possessions what sort of damage are your possessions protected against?

3 What is the minimum cost of insuring a bicycle, for
   a) a month?   *b)* a year?

4 You have insured your camera with an All Risks policy.
   a) What is your camera protected against?
   b) In what part of the world will your All Risks insurance policy be valid?
   c) Would you get any money back from the policy if your camera was stolen from a car?

5 How much could you be paid if you fall off the bike that you have insured and hurt yourself badly?

8.7 Check your knowledge of language.

1 What does the phrase 'valid for one calendar month' mean?

2 In some parts of the policy the word 'certain' is used. For example, the policy covers your possessions against '… certain fire, theft… etc.' What effect does this word 'certain' have on the meaning?

8.8 *Listen to the talk in the Teacher's File.*

TRF
PAGE 85–87

8.9

Read the passage that follows. The writer, Mike Brace, became blind after the accident described below.

Remember, remember

When I came round, I was lying on the grass, with the smell of burnt flesh and gunpowder in my nostrils and a warm sticky liquid trickling down my face. For a second or two I could not work out what had happened, but when I put my hand to my face and saw
5 my palm covered in blood, I remembered, and realized that I was badly cut.

I had been playing football on the local common in Hackney, near my home in East London, when I had seen a small group of boys huddled together looking at something on the ground. As the
10 ball went out of play I ran to where they were gathered and arrived just as they were moving away. On the ground, and the object of their attention, was a black medicine bottle with the lid screwed on tight. I bent and picked the bottle up and was reading the label, when it exploded in my face. I remember hearing
15 someone say, 'Drop it!' but had taken no notice until it was too late. The date was Wednesday 2nd of November 1960, and the cause of the explosion, a banger inside the bottle.

I rose to my feet and began to run home, my friends racing along with me and I remember an old lady saying, 'Have you cut 20 yourself son?'

My reply was none too polite for a ten-year-old lad. It was something like, 'No, I have always had blood running down my face you silly old…'

As I entered my street I remember seeing my aunt on the 25 doorstep talking to a neighbour. I pushed past her and into the kitchen, where I filled a basin with cold water and plunged my face into it. It was then, I think, that I realized just how serious my injuries were. The water turned immediately a very dark red and no matter how many times I emptied the basin and put my face in, 30 the water continued to turn red.

At that point a neighbour came into the kitchen to look at the cuts. His alarm was obvious, and he offered at once to take me to the hospital. At this point I could still see normally and thought that I had just cut myself badly.

Slightly adapted from *Where There's a Will* by Mike Brace.
Mike is now a social worker and a keen sportsperson.

8.10

Answer all the questions that follow.

1 How did the accident happen?

2 What details in the text make it clear that Mike is badly hurt?

3 Was anyone to blame?

4 Why do you think the chapter heading is 'Remember, remember'? There are two reasons for this.

5 How do you think the boys who had left the bottle in the field felt?

8.11

SKILLS
PAGE 119–121

OPTIONS

1 Imagine that you are the aunt of Mike Brace. The children with the firework were only ten years old. You are very angry because a lot of shops in your area are selling fireworks to children who are too young. Write a letter to your local newspaper. Explain what happened. Give your views.

2 Imagine that you are one of the boys who had put the firework in the bottle. Write your diary entry for the day of the accident. Say what happened and how you felt.

The TV stunt that was too hot to handle

VIEWERS watched stunned as one of Italy's favourite TV hosts was set ablaze during an unusual stunt. Gabriella Carlucci was supposed to emerge from the flames after a car dragged her at 50mph over a blazing road. But she lost her grip on the cable and came to a halt as fire raged around her.

Studio workers sprayed her with foam and dragged her to safety. A bruised, shocked but unburned Miss Carlucci still managed to smile for the cameras, telling viewers: "I'm so sorry to frighten you but there was a little error."

She promised that her regular Trial of Courage on the programme *Buona Domenica* (Happy Sunday) would continue.

Fans of the weekly show have seen her bungee-jump from a skyscraper and crash a car head-on.

"I'm going to do a lot more for you, but I won't tell you what it is yet," she added.

A confident smile before the stunt

Blazing host: Gabriella Carlucci tries to fight off the flames

From the *Daily Mail*

8.12

Read the article on page 76, then answer the questions below.

1 What is Miss Carlucci's job?

2 Explain in your own words what happened to Miss Carlucci or draw and label a diagram or make a picture board to show what happened.

3 What is the Italian word for Sunday?

4 Which word in the first paragraph tells the reader that Gabriella was meant to have no problems with the stunt?

5 *a)* Which word is used by the writer of the article to describe how the viewers felt when they saw the accident happening?

   b) Which word did Miss Carlucci use to describe how she thought the audience felt when they saw the accident?

   c) Which of the two words in *a* and *b* do you think best describes how you would feel if you had seen the accident?

8.13

Use the information from the extract on pages 74 and 75 to make a report for a newspaper like the one opposite. Use your own ideas or the ones here.

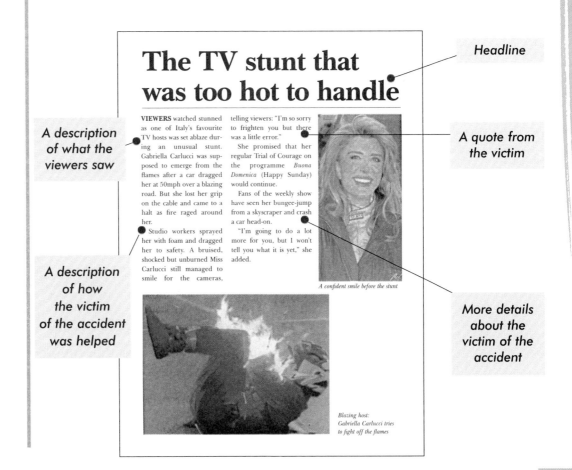

Headline

The TV stunt that was too hot to handle

A description of what the viewers saw

VIEWERS watched stunned as one of Italy's favourite TV hosts was set ablaze during an unusual stunt. Gabriella Carlucci was supposed to emerge from the flames after a car dragged her at 50mph over a blazing road. But she lost her grip on the cable and came to a halt as fire raged around her.

Studio workers sprayed her with foam and dragged her to safety. A bruised, shocked but unburned Miss Carlucci still managed to smile for the cameras, telling viewers: "I'm so sorry to frighten you but there was a little error."

She promised that her regular Trial of Courage on the programme *Buona Domenica* (Happy Sunday) would continue.

Fans of the weekly show have seen her bungee-jump from a skyscraper and crash a car head-on.

"I'm going to do a lot more for you, but I won't tell you what it is yet," she added.

A quote from the victim

A confident smile before the stunt

A description of how the victim of the accident was helped

More details about the victim of the accident

Blazing host: Gabriella Carlucci tries to fight off the flames

8.14 Read the poem. It is about the football accident at Hillsborough in 1989 where over 90 football fans died.

The bell

The bell
tolled all afternoon
we did not send to ask
for whom.
It told of flowers
heaped in a goalmouth,
red and blue scarves
heaped together at an altar;
it told of
eyes like TV screens
haunted by last night's images
tears dried by the April wind.
As the flags at half-mast
stirred overhead
the deep bell
still tolled in our heads
long after the light had gone.

Adrian Henri

tolled – the sound of a large bell; the sound is made to warn or tell people of something

altar – a place of worship

8.15

Answer these questions.

1 What message is the tolling bell giving?

2 What word in the poem makes the same sound as 'tolled'?

3 What words and phrases tell the reader that the people who saw the accident will not forget it for a long time?

4 Explain why some images haunt people. In what ways do they do this?

5 Which words and phrases describe mourning?

6 How do you feel when you read this poem?

7 Adrian Henri wrote a poem about the accident, because he is a poet. What other ways can we remind ourselves about accidents and how dreadful they were at the time?

Getting together

Mr L. Hill and Mrs J. Shaw
have great pleasure in inviting

Chris Robbins

to the marriage of their daughter

Jane

to

Daniel Chapter

at
St John's Church, Burton,
on
September 4th at 11 a.m.

and to the reception afterwards which will be
held at St John's Hall

Oak House
Salter Avenue
Portsmouth
PO8 7QD

R.S.V.P.

St – stands for **S**ain**t**

a reception – a meal for the people invited to the wedding

R.S.V.P. – please reply to the invitation. It stands for
Répondez **s**'il **v**ous **p**laît (reply if you please)

9.1

Read the wedding invitation on page 80, then answer the questions.

1 What is the name of the person who has been invited to the wedding?

2 Where is the wedding to take place?

3 What date is the wedding?

4 What time does the wedding start?

5 What will Jane's name be when she is married?

6 Whereabouts do you think St John's Hall might be?

7 Why do you think the mother and father of Jane have got different surnames?

9.2

SKILLS
PAGE 119

SKILLS
PAGES 120–121

OPTIONS

1 You are going to be on holiday in Spain on the date of the wedding. Write a letter to say you will not be able to go. Use your own name and address.

   Draw and address the envelope.

2 You have ordered some plates, cups and saucers as a wedding present. They arrive to you with two plates broken. You are surprised to see that there is very little packing in the box to protect the set.

   Write a letter asking for two more plates. They were in the Autumn Leaf Design.

   The address is: Glenfield Consumer Services, PO Box 78, Croydon CP2 9FR.

9.3

In a group discuss what you think is most important in a best friend.
Read the list below and put into the order of importance, e.g. C =1.

A Always tells the truth

B Always keeps a promise

C Will lend you money and not hurry to get it back

D Keeps a secret

E Sticks up for you, even if you are in the wrong

F Shares clothes

G Will help you out if you are in trouble

9.4

Listen to the announcement in the Teacher's File. Then jot down the details you need to remember.

TRF

PAGE 89

9.5 Read the details below. They come from a local newspaper.

BIRTHS

HOPKINS - Ben and Nikki
(née Martin)
are pleased
to announce the birth of

Mark Jon

on February 4th, 1996
at Bank Hospital.
A brother for Jack, Amanda and Jenni.

The first name, in capitals, is the surname of the family
née – born as; the surname that a woman was born with

9.6 Write down the sentences below. Fill in the blanks.

1 The first names of the new baby are - - - - and - - -.

2 The surname of the new baby is - - - - - - -.

3 The new baby has - - - sisters and - - - brother.

4 The father's full name is - - - - - - - - -.

5 The mother's full married name is - - - - - - - - - - - - .

6 Before the mother married her full name was - - - - - - - - - - -.

7 The baby's birthday is on - - - - - - - - -th.

B. Cert.
S.R./R.B.D.

CAUTION—It is an offence to falsify a certificate or to make or knowingly use a false certificate or a copy of a false certificate intending it to be accepted as genuine to the prejudice of any person or to possess a certificate knowing it to be false without lawful authority.

CERTIFIED COPY OF AN ENTRY
Pursuant to the Births and Deaths Registration Act 1953

NHS Number	YK350LI91	BIRTH	ENTRY No.	186

| Registration district | Wessex | Administrative area | |
| Sub-district | Grantchester | Wessex | |

1. Date and place of birth — CHILD
Tenth September 1996. General Hospital, Grantchester

2. Name and surname — Lisa Jane BROWN

3. Sex — Female

4. Name and surname — FATHER — John Adam BROWN

5. Place of birth — Grantchester

6. Occupation — Driving Instructor

7. Name and Surname — MOTHER — Alison BROWN

8. Place of birth — Barchester

9. (a) Maiden name — SMITH
(b) Surname at marriage if different from maiden surname —

10. Usual address (if different from place of child's birth) — 10 The Drive, Grantchester.

INFORMANT
11. Name and surname (if not the mother or father) —
12. Qualification — Father Mother

13. Usual address (if different from that in 10 above) —

14. I certify that the particulars entered above are true to the best of my knowledge and belief
John A. Brown
Signature of Informant

15. Date of registration — Seventeenth September 1996

16. Signature of registrar — Alfred Bunbury

Certified to be a true copy of an entry in a register in my custody.

Alfred Bunbury
ALFRED BUNBURY Registrar

17th Sept '96 SP 897123
Date

NHS – National Health Service
occupation – on this form, a job
maiden surname – surname that a woman uses before
  marriage
to certify – on this form, to say in writing

9.7

Use the details on the birth certificate to answer the questions below.

1 What is the name of the baby on the birth certificate?

2 When was the baby born?

3 Where do the baby's parents live?

4 What was the mother's full name before she was married?

5 Where was the mother born?

6 What job does the father do?

7 On what date was the birth registered?

9.8

SEE ALSO
PAGE 83

SKILLS
PAGE 127

OPTIONS

1 Write the notice of this birth for the local newspaper.
   Look at page 83 to help you.

2 Imagine the parents of the baby are friends of yours. Write a
   short note of congratulations to them. See page 127 if you
   need help.

3 Write ten tips to help someone live with a new baby in the
   family. You could make it into a chart and illustrate it.

9.9 | Read the poem below.

My crime

Unlike my brother I did not die young.

I had fits and croup, caused sleepless nights
and trips to clinics.

My feet outgrew shoes which cost money
and I was no beauty.

I answered back, stayed out and was ungrateful.
People washed their hands of me (more than once).

Unlike me my brother died young
golden-haired, one week old, in an incubator.

Angela McSeveney

croup – childhood illness that makes it hard to
breathe and causes a loud, ringing cough
incubator – machine that helps to keep poorly babies alive

9.10 | Answer these questions about the poem.

1 Verses 2, 3 and 4 describe the person in the poem at
different ages. Say how old you think the person was in
each of the verses.

2 Name three of the complaints made about the person
in the poem.

3 Why do you think no one complained about the brother?

4 How does the person in the poem feel about their brother?
Why do you think this?

5 The title of the poem is 'My crime'. What is the 'crime'?

6 Does the girl or boy in the poem think the parents do
not love them? Do you think she/he is right?

7 Is the person in the poem a girl or a boy?
Say why you think this.

9.11

Work in groups of three or four.

1 Pick one of the problems A–E below, to discuss.

2 Choose someone in the group to jot down the ideas you have.

3 In your group work out all the tips and advice you could give to help with the problem.

4 Pick someone in your group to tell the other groups what you have discussed.

5 Ask the other groups to add to your ideas.

A What should you do if you like someone very much, but do not know if they want to go out with you?

B Your friends are trying to persuade you to do something that you do not want to do. They say you are too scared to do it, that you are a chicken, that you are a baby, etc. What advice can you give to someone in that position?

C Your best mate is going out with someone who you know is no good. What should you do about it?

D Someone is spreading a lot of lies about you. Your friends are beginning to think there is some truth in them. What can you do?

E All your friends seem to have more money than you. You are beginning to feel embarrassed about your clothes and the fact you can't buy the things that they do. What advice could you give to someone in that position?

9.12

SEE ALSO
PAGES 20, 56

TRF
PAGES 41–42

1 Write a DO and DON'T chart for teenagers that gives advice about a problem/problems. (See pages 20 and 56 for ideas.)

2 Write and design a leaflet for teenagers that gives advice about a problem.
   You will find more information on writing leaflets in the Teacher's Resource File.

9.13

In the extract that follows Roger and Cindy are going away for a few days' holiday. They are leaving their two teenage daughters alone on the farm.

Work as a class or in a group and read paragraphs A–F.
At the end of EACH paragraph discuss:

1 What do you think will happen next?
2 Why do you think this?

PAGES 90–91

Paragraphs A–F are also available in the Teacher's Resource File.

Time to go

A

It was the eagerness in their eyes that Roger kept thinking about as he and Cindy drove north towards Grand Rapids Thursday evening, and how pleasant the girls were, how helpful as they saw their parents out to the car. "Here, Dad, let me carry that. In you go. Okay, you two have a good time and don't worry about us." Driving north he could hear Cathy's voice saying, "Don't worry about us, don't worry about us," . . .

B

. . . and just north of Aitkin he turned around and headed south.
"Are you crazy?" Cindy said.
"Yes," he said – "as a father of two teenage daughters, I'd be crazy not to be crazy."

C

When they turned onto the county road a half-mile east of their place, they noticed more cars than you normally see, all heading west. They came over the hill. Up ahead, their house was blazing with lights. All the traffic was turning in at their driveway. They could hear the music quite clearly from the road as they cruised past.

D

"You don't want to go in?" she said. Roger said, "I don't know. Maybe it's something we don't want to know about."
"Then let's turn around and forget we ever saw this, whatever it is. God help us, I hope it isn't what we think," she said.
At the crossroads, he parked on the shoulder and they got out and looked at the farm. Across the muddy field, with so much standing water the house looked like a cruise ship with a big party on board. More cars drove up the gangplank.
"Probably it's not what we think," she said. "If we're going to trust them, then we have to trust them and not go around spying on them to see if they do what we want or not."

E

"I'm curious. I'm going over to see what's going on. Want to come?"

"Of course I do," she said.

It was hard going. They took off their shoes and socks and waded through the mud up to their ankles, straight across the field in the dark, towards the carnival in their farmyard. Headlights, loud music: he didn't know there were this many teenage kids in the county. They got to the edge of the windbreak. It didn't seem like their place with the music blasting. Voices screeching, drums pounding.

Roger peeked around the corner of the coop. Kids milled around, went in the house, came out. More cars pulled up, kids got out. Two kegs of beer by the back door. Kids moved around, restless hanging around, watching other kids hanging around, watching to see if there was more fun somewhere else, boys circling, girls waiting – a lot like a party he sort of remembered from twenty-five years or so ago . . .

Some kids lit cigarettes, took long drags, big clouds of smoke. Lighting up – Roger remembered that. Kids passing their cigarettes round. That's generous, he thought. And there was his own little girl, Martha – reaching for a cigarette . . . No! No! he thought. Don't. She put it in her mouth, his sweet little daughter. Oh darling child don't. A boy lit it and out of her sweet lips came smoke. Roger had taken two steps out from behind the coop. He wanted to run to her and yet he really didn't.

F

Cindy was right behind him, her hand on his back. "This is ridiculous. I can't believe they'd do this. Are we going to allow this?"

"I don't know."

"You don't? No? Well. I don't know either," she said. "I was hoping you'd know. You're always so – so –"

"Strict?"

"Yes."

"You know something?" he said. "I'm getting tired of being a dad." He didn't want to be a cop, have everybody get quiet and him make a speech while sullen kids slink away cursing him under their breath. He wanted to take his lovely wife by her cool hand – Come away, come away, my love, my sweet slim darling, mother of my children, come away . . .

She said "Look! They're trampling on my petunias."

"Come," he said.

"You're just going to walk away and leave them?"

"Yes."

"Are you sure this is right?"

"No."

From *Leaving Home* by Garrison Keillor

9.14

Answer the questions below.

1 What do the girls say and do that make Roger feel that his daughters want him and his wife to go away? (Use your own words.) (A)

2 Why do you think the girls want their parents out of the way?

3 What does Roger decide to do in the second paragraph? (B)

4 Make a list of what Roger and Cindy see and hear when they get back to their house. (C, D, E)

5 Do you think Roger and Cindy will 'walk away'? Say why. (F)

6 Make a list of some of the things that might happen if they stopped the party. Now make a list of some of the things that might happen if they 'walk away'.

7 Do you think they should 'walk away'? Say why.

9.15 A couple are thinking of getting married or living together. Make a list of all the practical things they need to think about when they decide to set up home together.

9.16 Read the poem below.

The passionate shepherd to his love

Come live with me, and be my love,
And we will all the pleasures prove,
That Vallies, groves, hills and fields,
Woods, or steepie mountain yields.

prove – try out
a **grove** – a small wood
yields – gives

And we will sit upon the Rocks
Seeing the Shepherds feed their flocks,
By shallow Rivers, to whose falls,
Melodious birds sing Madrigals.

falls – waterfalls
Melodious – tuneful
Madrigals – songs

And I will make thee beds of Roses,
And a thousand fragrant posies,
A cap of flowers, and a kirtle,
Embroidered all with leaves of Mirtle.

thee – you
fragrant – sweet smelling
a **kirtle** – a skirt

A gown made of the finest wool,
Which from our pretty Lambs we pull,
Fair linèd slippers for the cold:
With buckles of the purest gold.

A belt of straw, and Ivy buds,
With Coral clasps and Amber studs,
And if these pleasures may thee move,
Come live with me, and be my love.

The Shepherds Swains shall dance and sing,
For thy delight each May-morning,
If these delights thy mind may move,
Then live with me, and be my love.

Swains – boys

Christopher Marlowe

9.17

Answer these questions about the poem.

1 What is the Shepherd asking his girlfriend to do?

2 *a)* What kind of bed is he offering to make for his girlfriend?
   b) What are the advantages and disadvantages of the bed?

3 *a)* Which verse has the most practical suggestions?
   b) Describe these practical suggestions in your own words.

4 *a)* Re-read verses 2 and 6. For each verse describe what the
      Shepherd says he and his girlfriend will be doing and
      seeing. Use your own words where possible.
   b) Now describe what the surroundings in verses 2
      and 6 will be like in winter.

5 What practical details has the Shepherd missed out?

9.18

OPTIONS

1 Write a letter of reply that the girlfriend might make
   to her lover.

2 Imagine the boy and girl decide to live together.
   Make a chart of tips and advice for a happy home.

3 **Men should not do the washing up, the cleaning, cooking,
   shopping or washing and ironing. That is a woman's job.**
   Discuss this. Do you agree? Give your reasons. Write your
   views with the aim of trying to persuade someone who does not
   agree with you OR give a short talk to your class on the subject.

Skills

Capital letters

Capital letters are used at the beginning of sentences, e.g.

Thank you for your letter.

10.1 Write out the passage below, putting in the capital letters at the beginning of each sentence.

rabbits need green food. they like carrot tops, grass and cabbage leaves. if possible give your rabbit fresh water in the morning and evening. clean out the cage as often as possible.

Capital letters are used for people's names and I, e.g.

Curtis **B**oswell, **I**

10.2 Write out the passage below, putting in the capital letters for the names and I.

i am writing to let you know that three more people would like to join the club. Their names are john white, melanie jacks and anita patell. There may be one more. jenny penn is still thinking about it.

Capital letters

Capital letters are used for the names of the week and months of the year, e.g.

Saturday, **M**arch

10.3 **Write out the passage below, putting in the capital letters for the days of the week and months of the year.**

Dear Mr Johns,

Thank you for your letter. I could come on saturday february 3rd or friday march 1st. If these dates are too late, I can take some time off and come down on wednesday january 31st.

Capital letters are used for the names of roads, e.g.

West **S**treet, **O**ak **A**venue, **B**arn **C**ross **R**oad

10.4 **Write out the passage below, putting in the capital letters for the names of roads.**

14 butler avenue
London
E10 5JN

John Betts
85 henley road   May 12th, 1996
Pitley
Beds
BF6 8SD

Dear Mr Betts,

This is to let you know that I will be changing my address on July 14th. The new address will be, 12, holme green close, Frinchurch, Sussex FS3 9SP.

Capital letters

Capital letters are used for the names of towns, counties and countries, e.g.

London, **B**edfordshire, **E**ngland

10.5 Write out the passage below, putting in the capital letters for the names of countries, towns and counties.

Hi everyone,

Well, here we are in spain. It's wonderful. The sea is blue and the weather's boiling. Not like france, germany and italy where it rained the whole time. Only two more days left then it's back to sheffield and work! Great!

Capital letters are used for the titles of books and newspapers and names, such as the name of an animal or house, e.g.

The **R**edcar **G**azette, **R**over, **G**reenways **H**ouse

10.6 Write out the sentences below, putting in the capital letters for the names of newspapers, books and other names.

1 The best place to look for a flat is in the watford times.
2 Our dog is called spot.
3 I have just finished reading 'animal farm'.
4 Did you see 'brookside' last night?
5 There's a barbecue at the king's head on Saturday.
6 The house is called rose cottage.

10.7 Test yourself on capital letters. You will find a test on page 102 of the Teacher's File.

TRF
PAGE 102

Sentences

Full stops or question marks (or other punctuation marks) are put at the end of sentences.

10.8

Write out the sentences below. Put in a full stop or a question mark at the end of each one.

1 How are you

2 I have applied for the job

3 What is your address

4 Don't forget to turn off the light

5 Where have you been

A sentence must make sense.

10.9

Read 1–9 below. Then write out the ones that are <u>sentences</u>. Put a full stop or a question mark at the end.

1 The house

2 I am very hot

3 Did you let the cat out

4 In the sitting room

5 A lot of fun

6 Write your answers on a postcard

7 For a cat

8 Did you post the letter

9 Black and white

Sentences

> Sentences must make sense.

10.10

Write out 1–7 below. Put in the full stop between the sentences. Do not forget the capital letter. Make sure both sentences make sense, e.g.

1 The man picked up the cat. It was almost dead.

1 The man picked up the cat it was almost dead.

2 It was too dark to see anything the girls hunted for the torch.

3 Water the pot plant in the evening keep it away from sunlight.

4 The boots cost twenty pounds they were too much money for Zak.

5 Gareth could not sleep rain was beginning to drip into the tent.

6 The dog barked the boy jumped out of bed and ran downstairs.

7 Put the egg in boiling water let it cook for four minutes.

10.11

Write out the passage below. Put in the full stops and capital letters. Remember that sentences must make sense. (Add five more full stops.)

The room was not too bad it needed painting here and there Paul went into the kitchen at first he thought it was all right then he spotted the marks on the walls water had been leaking down from the flat upstairs.

10.12

TRF
PAGE 99

Test yourself on sentences. You will find a test on page 99 of the Teacher's File.

Sentences

> Sentences must make sense.

10.13

Write out sentences 1–6 below. Put in the full stops between the sentences. Do not forget the capital letters. Make sure all THREE sentences make sense, e.g.

1 It was very cold. The old lady filled up a hot water bottle and went to bed. Even with three more blankets she still could not get warm.

1 It was very cold the old lady filled up a hot water bottle and went to bed even with three more blankets she still could not get warm.

2 Stir the paint before you begin then only put a small amount of paint on your brush it is best if you start painting at the top of the wall.

3 Thank you for your letter I am pleased to say that I will be able to come in March by then I am hoping to have a car.

4 The train was two hours late all the shops on the platform were shut there was nowhere for us to get a hot drink.

5 Put the water in the saucepan when the water begins to boil add the carrot put a lid on the pan and leave for five minutes.

6 Tell the milkman we will not need any milk for a week stop the papers for two weeks give the spare key to Mrs Tebbs and tell her to keep an eye on the house.

10.14

Write out the passage below. Put in the capital letters and six missing full stops. Remember that sentences must make sense.

It does not cost a lot of money to feed birds nuts or breadcrumbs rolled in a little bit of fat make good food some birds like blue tits hang from a net and peck at nuts other birds like robins and starlings eat from the ground that is when you need to keep a look out for a cat some cats hide behind a bush waiting for the birds to be fed then they pounce.

Speech marks

In a comic, when someone speaks, their words are put into speech bubbles.

In a story, speech marks are used instead, e.g.

"Hello," said Jon.

10.15

Write out the sentences below, putting in the speech marks. Copy the sentence carefully. Do not miss out commas, full stops or question marks.

1 Hello, Jon said.

2 What is the time? asked Bertha.

3 See you tomorrow, Callum yelled.

4 What is your dog called? Mr Chubb asked.

5 Don't make a noise, whispered Petra.

6 Do you want chips with that? Mr Ming asked.

7 Wayne looked at the letter, It's from Jim, he said.

Speech marks

When more than one person is talking, start a new line when each person speaks.

10.16

Match the questions with the answers. Put the question on one line and the answer on another line. Add the speech marks. The first one has been done for you.

"When is the next bus?" asked Tim.
"At two o'clock," he said.

QUESTIONS	ANSWERS
When is the next bus? asked Tim	In the top flat, Phil said.
How old are you? Sam asked.	Baked beans, yelled Tom.
Where does Jenny live? Pat asked.	At two o'clock, he said.
How much does it cost? Murray asked.	Seventy, Mrs Hoyle said.
Who is that over there? asked Glenn.	One pound, groaned Sam.
What do you want to eat? Bob asked.	Jack Roberts, Karen said.

Speech marks

> When someone speaks, a comma or question mark – or other punctuation mark – comes afterwards. This comma or question mark comes **inside** the speech marks, e.g.
>
>   "Where are you going?" she asked.

10.17

Write out the sentences below. Put a comma or question mark where there is a line.

1 "Fetch the paper from the shops_ " Kevin said.

2 "Why did you do that_ " Mrs Woods said crossly.

3 "Where's my money_ " asked Sam.

4 "We've got five minutes before the bus goes_ " Sian said.

5 "It's not here_ " she said, lifting up the mat.

6 "What have you done to your hand_ " Matthew asked.

7 "What do you call that_ " asked Dean.

10.18

Test yourself on speech marks.

TRF PAGE 105

Speech marks

When two people are talking, start a new line for each person, e.g.

> "What is the time?" he asked.
>
> "Four o'clock," she said.

10.19

Write out the sentences below, putting in the speech marks.

1 Where are you going? Martin asked.
To the shops, Tim said.

2 I've got the tickets for the match, Nikki grinned.
That's great, Viv said.

3 Where is the nearest garage? Mr Shahid asked.
Turn left at the traffic lights, the woman said.

10.20

Copy the passage below, putting in the speech marks.

Phil started cleaning the bikes. They were really filthy after the long ride.

Hey, Jan. How about a cup of tea? he yelled.

Get it yourself, Jan shouted.

Phil sat down. He had been cleaning the bikes for two hours. What had Jan been doing all morning?

Oh come on, Jan, he yelled.

I'm not here to run around after you all day! Jan screamed back.

Well, that did it. Phil picked up the bowl full of water and tipped it down the drain.

If you can't make me a cup of tea, he yelled, then I can't clean the bikes.

Paragraphs

A paragraph is usually a number of sentences about one topic. Very often the first sentence says what the topic will be.

10.21

The first sentence of each of the paragraphs below has been taken out. Work out which sentences A–D should start each paragraph, e.g.

Paragraph 1 starts with sentence C.

1 _____ If you are young or old, keen on sport or just want to chat to your friends, this leisure centre is for you. Bad weather cannot spoil your fun here. Play golf all the year round, sit in our garden in mid-winter and try boating on our indoor lake in the middle of January.

2 _____ We have all the usual activities such as tennis, squash and badminton, as well as some you might not expect. People travel over fifty miles to come to our two dry ski slopes, and the ice skating rinks are the largest in the county.

3 _____ We have some of the best experts to help you. We will check your health first. Then we will give you your own exercise plan. The leisure centre has everything you will need to get in top form, from exercise bikes to treadmills and weight lifting.

4 _____ The leisure centre is for you too. We have rest rooms, television rooms and a cinema complex. For those who enjoy card games there are bridge and whist rooms. Tiny tots and the not so tiny tots can enjoy the play rooms and theme areas.

The sentences

A Some people just want to get out of the house and enjoy themselves.

B We have plenty for those who want to get fit but do not want to do sports.

C Kinton Leisure Centre has something for everyone.

D If you are keen on sport, then no one can offer you more than we do.

Paragraphs

A paragraph is usually a number of sentences about one topic. Very often the first sentence says what the topic will be.

10.22 The first sentence of each paragraph below has been taken out. Work out which sentence A–D should start each paragraph.

1 _____ I do not like dangerous dogs and I would not like to meet a bull in a field. However, these are not things that usually happen, luckily. I hate snakes but then I have only seen them in zoos. I think the one thing I really do not like are spiders, and where I live spiders seem to be hiding everywhere.

2 _____ They move so fast. When I am asleep I can actually hear them as they scuttle across the wall near my head. Where I live, we get really large spiders with long hairy legs and big thick bodies. It makes me shudder just thinking about them.

3 _____ The outside wall of the house that we rent, is covered with ivy. Spiders love ivy, I am sure of it. There is a small garden at the back. In the winter the dead leaves and twigs are just where spiders like to live. Inside the house there are all sorts of cupboards and small holes that they can creep into.

4 _____ What I want is a lovely modern flat. Outside all I want to see are pavements and streets. It would be good to have a tree nearby, as long as it is quite a few metres away from where I live.

The sentences

A The trouble is we live in the country.

B There are not many things I am frightened of.

C I have made up my mind I am going to move into town.

D Spiders really terrify me.

Paragraphs

A paragraph is usually a number of sentences about one topic. Very often the first sentence says what the topic will be.

10.23

The passage below has not been split into paragraphs. Write out the passage splitting it into four paragraphs.

Outside the tent the rain lashed down. Tim hunted for the torch in the dark. He had left the windows of the van open. If he didn't shut them soon, the seats would be soaked. Tim pulled on a jacket. He crawled out of the tent and looked round. He was surprised to find it wasn't too dark. The full moon made everywhere look silver. Tim could even see his shadow on the ground. The trees waved in the wind. You could see the moon reflected in the puddles. Tim made a dash to the van. Then he got a shock. One of the doors was open. That was odd. He was sure he hadn't left a door open. Then he spotted the shadow. It stretched out in front of the van. Someone was there. Tim began to back away slowly. He must get to the tent and wake the others. If he was quick, all four of them could rush to the van. They might just be in time to stop anyone from taking it away.

10.24

TRF
PAGE 109

There are more activities on paragraphs in the Teacher's File.

Plurals

To make most nouns plural (more than one) add an 's'.

cup ———▶ cup**s**

10.25

Write out the sentences below making the underlined words plural, e.g.

1 The <u>cups</u> crashed to the floor.

1 The <u>cup</u> crashed to the floor.
2 Before going out, Tom locked the <u>door.</u>
3 The <u>girl</u> climbed up the ladder.
4 I can't find my <u>key</u>.
5 Ask for a timetable when you get the <u>ticket</u>.
6 The <u>light</u> went out in the storm.

Add '**es**' to words ending in '**ss**' '**s**' '**ch**' '**sh**' '**x**' to make them plural.

bo**x** ———▶ bo**xes**

10.26

Write out the sentences below adding 'es' to the underlined words, e.g.

1 Put the <u>boxes</u> in the shed, please.

1 Put the <u>box</u> in the shed, please.
2 The man looked at the <u>scratch</u> on his arm.
3 We watched the <u>fox</u> playing in the moonlight.
4 You can't get on the <u>bus</u> very well if you are in a wheelchair.
5 Put the <u>glass</u> on the top shelf.
6 Don't leave your tooth <u>brush</u> in the sink.

Plurals

When words end in one **'f'** or **'fe'** take off the **'f'** or **'fe'** and add **'ves'** to make them plural.

calf ⟶ cal**ves**   wi**fe** ⟶ wi**ves**

10.27

Write out the sentences below making the underlined words plural, e.g.

1 They watched the <u>calves</u> being sold in the market.

1 They watched the <u>calf</u> being sold in the market.
2 Wash the <u>shelf</u> before you put any more food out.
3 The <u>wolf</u> prowled round the cage.
4 Put the <u>loaf</u> on the bottom shelf.
5 The <u>knife</u> clattered to the floor.
6 The gardener looked at the <u>leaf</u>.

To make some words ending in **'o'** plural add **'es'**.

tomat**o** ⟶ tomato**es**

10.28

Write out the sentences below adding 'es' to the underlined words, e.g.

1 I don't want any <u>tomatoes</u> in my salad.

1 I don't want any <u>tomato</u> in my salad.
2 I like my <u>potato</u> with lots of butter.
3 Listen to the <u>echo</u> in this cave.
4 If you go for a holiday in Scotland, beware of the <u>mosquito</u>.
5 The street gave a party when the <u>hero</u> returned.
6 They watched the pictures of the burning <u>volcano</u>.

Plurals

When words end in a consonant and a 'y', take off the 'y' and add 'ies'.

baby ⟶ bab**ies**

10.29

Write out the sentences below making the underlined words plural, e.g.

1 The nurse dressed the <u>babies</u>.

> 1 The nurse dressed the <u>baby</u>.
> 2 Tell the <u>lady</u> to come this way.
> 3 He checked the speed of the <u>lorry</u>.
> 4 The <u>fly</u> buzzed round the room.
> 5 I liked to feed the <u>pony</u> in the field.
> 6 Mrs Cliff will answer your <u>enquiry</u>.

10.30

Check your spelling of plurals. Write out the sentences below making the underlined words plural, e.g.

1 You can see the <u>hills</u> from the window.

> 1 You can see the <u>hill</u> from the window.
> 2 You have dropped the <u>domino</u> on the floor.
> 3 Get some more batteries for the <u>torch</u>.
> 4 The boys sat on the <u>bench</u> in the park.
> 5 I would like to look at the <u>scarf</u> on the top shelf.
> 6 Will the <u>family</u> with young children go in the front coach.

10.31

Test yourself on more spellings. You will find a test on page 110 of the Teacher's File.

Doubling rule – adding 'ed' and 'ing'

> When short words end in **one vowel** and **one consonant** (except **w, x** or **y**) double the final consonant when adding **'ed'** or **'ing'**.
>
> stop ——→ stop**ped**

10.32

Write out the sentences below. Fill in each blank using the words in brackets but adding 'ed', e.g.

1 She <u>stopped</u> the car and jumped out.　(stop)

1 She _____ the car and jumped out.　(stop)
2 "Please can I go to the party?" Zati _____ .　(beg)
3 The black shoes _____ very well.　(fit)
4 They had _____ to catch the train.　(plan)
5 The man _____ the bag and ran.　(drop)
6 The boy _____ the dog.　(hug)

10.33

Write out the sentences below. Fill in each blank using the words in brackets but adding 'ing', e.g.

1 The boys were <u>sitting</u> at the back.　(sit)

1 The boys were _____ at the back.　(sit)
2 They were _____ as fast as they could.　(run)
3 She had been _____ the garden all morning.　(dig)
4 The boy stormed out, _____ the door as he went.　(slam)
5 Water was _____ all over the floor.　(drip)
6 "That hurt," she said, _____ her leg.　(rub)

Doubling rule – adding 'ed' and 'ing'

> When short words end in **one vowel** and **one consonant** (except **w, x** or **y**) double the final consonant when adding **'ed'** or **'ing'**.
>
> stop ⟶ stop**ped**

10.34

Write out the sentences below. Fill in each blank using the words in brackets but adding 'ed', e.g.

1 He <u>tripped</u> over the edge of the carpet.   (trip)

1 He _____ over the edge of the carpet.   (trip)

2 The road was _____ yesterday.   (grit)

3 The dog _____ his tail.   (wag)

4 She _____ the poster to the wall.   (pin)

5 He _____ the mark with a damp cloth.   (rub)

6 They _____ the dustbin to the top of the road.   (drag)

7 They _____ the bike to the back of the car.   (strap)

10.35

Write out the sentences below. Fill in each blank using the words in brackets but adding 'ing', e.g.

1 It is <u>getting</u> very cold outside.   (get)

1 It is _____ very cold outside.   (get)

2 "Do stop _____ ," she sighed.   (nag)

3 She will be _____ the carpet tomorrow.   (fit)

4 Everyone has been _____ on that patch of ice.   (slip)

5 The child could not stop _____ .   (sob)

6 This hedge needs _____ .   (trim)

7 "Get out quickly," he said, _____ the baby.   (grab)

Doubling rule – adding 'er' and 'est'

When short words end in **one vowel** and **one consonant** (except **w, x** or **y**) double the final consonant when adding **'er'** or **'est'**.

stop ⟶ stop**per**

10.36

Write out the sentences below. Fill in each blank using the words in brackets but adding 'er', e.g.

1 "I am the <u>winner</u>!" he shouted.   (win)

1 "I am the _____ !" he shouted.   (win)

2 He is a fast _____ . (run)

3 Can I borrow your _____ ?   (rub)

4 She is a really good _____ .   (swim)

5 Isn't that the _____ from the band?   (drum)

6 "Do you think I'm getting _____ ?" Chris asked. (thin)

10.37

Write out the sentences below. Fill in each blank using the words in brackets but adding 'est', e.g.

1 That is the <u>biggest</u> balloon I've ever seen.   (big)

1 That is the _____ balloon I've ever seen.   (big)

2 This has been the _____ summer since 1845.   (wet)

3 She is the _____ person I have ever seen.   (fat)

4 "It was the _____ day of my life," he whispered.   (sad)

5 Jake is the _____ person in this class.   (fit)

6 This is the _____ curry I have had.   (hot)

Adding 'ed' and 'ing'

When short words have **two vowels** in the middle or **two consonants** at the end, just add **'ed'** or **'ing'**.

sleep ⟶ sleep**ing**   jump ⟶ jump**ing**

10.38

Write out the sentences below. Fill each blank using the words in brackets but adding 'ed', e.g.

1 He <u>jumped</u> out of bed.   (jump)

1 He _____ out of bed.   (jump)

2 I _____ everywhere for the cat.   (look)

3 The car _____ into the lorry.   (crash)

4 "I've lost a pound," Robert _____ .   (groan)

5 When you have _____ your room, you can do mine. (paint)

When the last three letters of a word are **a vowel**, **a consonant** and **a silent 'e'**, knock off the **'e'** when adding **'ing'**, e.g.

hope ⟶ hop**ing**

10.39

Write out the sentences below. Fill in each blank with the words in brackets but adding 'ing', e.g.

1 I was <u>hoping</u> we would see you today.   (hope)

1 I was _____ we would see you today.   (hope)

2 Are you _____ to the disco next week?   (come)

3 "You must be _____ ," Aktar said.   (joke)

4 I hate _____ to get up at seven in the morning.   (have)

5 Do you mind _____ your feet when you come in.   (wipe)

6 "Stop _____ at me," she snapped.   (stare)

Adding 'ly'

> Most words do not change if 'ly' is added to them.
>
> love ——————> love**ly**

10.40

Write out the sentences below. Fill in each blank using the words in brackets and adding 'ly', e.g.

1 That looks <u>lovely</u>.   (love)

1 That looks _____ .   (love)
2 You will need to watch _____ .   (close)
3 Have you seen Sarah _____ ?   (late)
4 I write very _____ .   (neat)
5 He works very _____ .   (quick)
6 You need to dress _____ for that job.   (smart)
7 Are you _____ to see Mr Pitt tomorrow?   (like)
8 If you write, 'Dear Mr Fen,' end the letter, 'Yours _____ '. (sincere)

10.41

Write out the sentences below. Fill in each blank using the words in brackets and adding 'ly'. Note: all the words already end in 'l', e.g.

1 I <u>usually</u> catch the seven o'clock train.   (usual)

1 I _____ catch the seven o'clock train.   (usual)
2 Pack the glasses _____ .   (careful)
3 If the letter begins, 'Dear Sir,' you end with, 'Yours _____ '.   (faithful)
4 Are you _____ going to the party?   (real)
5 Did he _____ offer to give you a lift?   (actual)
6 I see you have _____ made up your mind.   (final)

Alphabetical order

Links with page 35

The list below are the names of the farmers whose details need to be put back into the filing cabinet. The filing cabinet drawers are numbered and labelled:

1 A–Com, 2 Con–Gor, 3 Gos–Jon, 4 Joo–Pag,
5 Pah–Rel, 6 Rem–Z.

10.42

Look at the drawers below and work out where each name should go. Take care to copy carefully and put in the capital letters where they should be. The first two names have been done for you:

F. Jolly = 3   H. Cummings = 2

F. Jolly	M. Gladwin	H. Thomas
H. Cummings	J.R. Rankin	J. Davies
O. Clegg	L. Padley	A. Horsley
B. M. Ashford	E. Williams	W. Perruzza

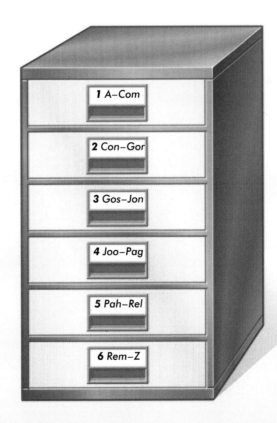

Alphabetical order

Links with page 35

10.43

Davis and Travers are re-organising their files. They want two filing cabinets, one for farmers and one for people who come to the vet with pets. Write down the names of the farmers only, putting the names in alphabetical order. Make sure you copy the names correctly and print the capital letters clearly. The first two have been done for you.

Farmers: B. Adams
            D. Allen

The list of names

S. Truss	C. Williams – Farmer
D. Allen – Farmer	H. Wong
J. F. Hill	M. Morris – Farmer
T. Simmonds	P. Tuffley – Farmer
P. Varley – Farmer	N. O'Shea
L. Harris – Farmer	T. Prunty – Farmer
B. Nakanda	P. White – Farmer
B. Plumb – Farmer	W. Stead
G. Kelly	B. Adams – Farmer

Alphabetical order

When two names are the same, then use the first name of the person to work out which goes first, e.g.

K. Jones goes before **M.** Jones

10.44

Below is a list of names. Put them in alphabetical order. When you write them down, make sure you copy the names carefully and write the capital letters clearly.

The list of names

L. Hollis

T. Scott

F. Moffatt

A. Esdale

R. Scott

M. Head

N. Yu

W. Brain

Alphabetical order

When two names start with the same letter, then use the second letter to work out which one goes first, e.g.

Ricks comes before **Ro**berts

If the first two letters of the name are the same then use the third letter to work out which goes first, e.g.

Roberts goes before **Roc**k

10.45

Below is a list of names that need to go into a filing cabinet. Put them in alphabetical order. When you write them down, make sure you copy the names carefully and write the capital letters clearly.

The list of names

Gilbert F.

Dunn J.

Roberts L.

King L.

Dutton B.

Rock D.

Platt R.

Gibbs R.

Ricks M.

Griffiths H.

Zia E.

Porter A.

General letter

Layout and details

24 Ardent Street
Wayford
Berks RG2 0KL
March 12th 1996

Public Transport
Hadley C. C.
Hadley
Berks RG4 NFH

Paragraph 1: *why you are writing*

Dear Mr Trafford,
I am writing to ask you whether you would consider running a bus to my area on Thursdays.

Paragraph 2: *giving background details*

I live on the Wayford Pass Housing Estate. This is a new estate which now has over a hundred houses on it. Before the housing estate there was no need for a bus. Now quite a large number of us would like to shop in Hadley at least once a week. As we do not have a car, some of us have been hiring a taxi on a Thursday so that we can go to the market.

Paragraph 3: *explaining what you want in detail*

I wondered whether the X26, which leaves Nattle at 9.25 and arrives in Hadley at ten o'clock, could call at Wayford on its way. It would only add another mile to the journey but I think there would be at least fourteen people using it on a Thursday. If the bus that leaves Hadley at 12.50 returned through Wayford it would give enough time to do the weekend shopping.

Paragraph 4: *final sentence saying what you hope will happen*

I do hope you will be able to help us.

Yours sincerely,

Chantra Harvey

Chantra Harvey

Letter of complaint

Links with pages 21, 45, 75, 81

Layout and details

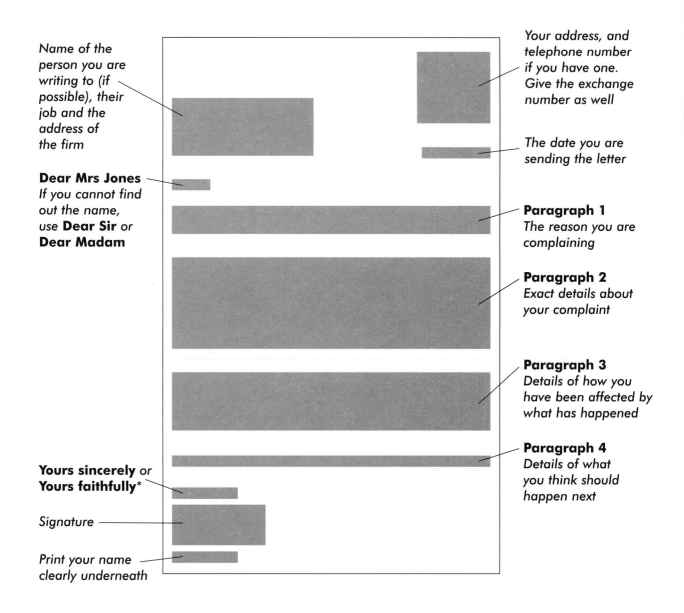

Name of the person you are writing to (if possible), their job and the address of the firm

Your address, and telephone number if you have one. Give the exchange number as well

The date you are sending the letter

Dear Mrs Jones
If you cannot find out the name, use **Dear Sir** or **Dear Madam**

Paragraph 1
The reason you are complaining

Paragraph 2
Exact details about your complaint

Paragraph 3
Details of how you have been affected by what has happened

Paragraph 4
Details of what you think should happen next

Yours sincerely or **Yours faithfully***

Signature

Print your name clearly underneath

*Use 'Yours sincerely' if you know the name, e.g. *Dear Mr Jenks* – end: *Yours sincerely*
Use 'Yours faithfully' if you do not know the name, e.g. *Dear Sir* – end: *Yours faithfully*

Letter of complaint

Links with pages 21, 45, 75, 81

Letter 1: *Complaining about a service or something you have bought*

28 Gordon Road
South Woodford
PO Box 683
London
E18 1DW

Consumer Services Department
Aroma Coffee
Swindon
SW5 8JK

May 18, 1996

Dear Sir,

I am writing to complain about a jar of your Four Star Aroma coffee granules.

I bought a 200g jar of the coffee from Gingham Stores, in Swindon, on May 16th. The *Best before* date was March 1999 and the *quality code number* was 501MRSR. When I opened the jar, I was very upset to find that most of the coffee was powdered, with just a few granules in it. It smelt very bitter and was impossible to drink. The seal had not been tampered with. I enclose a small amount for your inspection.

I am particularly annoyed because I had chosen your coffee as a special treat to use after a small dinner party I was giving. When it became obvious that it was impossible to drink, I was upset and embarrassed.

I would like an apology and a refund, at the very least.

Yours faithfully,

Tim Smart

Tim Smart

Job application

Layout and details

Name of the person you are writing to (if possible), their job and the address of the firm

Dear Mrs Jones
If you cannot find out the name, use **Dear Sir** *or* **Dear Madam**

Yours sincerely *or* **Yours faithfully***

Signature

Print your name clearly underneath

Your address, and telephone number if you have one. Give the exchange number as well

The date you are sending the letter

Paragraph 1
The reasons you are writing

Paragraph 2
Give details of work experience

Paragraph 3
Give some details about yourself and what you can offer

Paragraph 4
Other details, e.g. references, when you could start work, etc.

*Use 'Yours sincerely' if you know the name, e.g. *Dear Mr Jenks* – end: *Yours sincerely*

Use 'Yours faithfully' if you do not know the name, e.g. *Dear Sir* – end: *Yours faithfully*

Job application

Links with page 35

Letter 1: writing on chance for a job
(not in reply to an advertisement)

14 North Road
Sittingbourne
Kent
ME10 7GH
Tel: 01795 465899

June 7th 1996

Miss J. King
Six Fields Nursery
4 Oak Avenue
Sittingbourne
Kent
ME10 3GH

Dear Miss King,

I am writing to ask if you are likely to need any helpers in your Nursery in the next few months.

I worked at ABC Nursery School for six weeks in the school holidays last year. My job was mainly with the three-year-old children, where I helped with play, music and sporting activities. I also sometimes help Dr Smith with her two children at weekends. I am nearly sixteen years old and waiting for my GCSE results. I love working with children and hope to take an evening course to get a Nursery Nursing qualification. I can play the piano up to Grade 4 and am still having lessons.

I would particularly like to work at your Nursery School and would wait for a vacancy if you think there might be one in the fairly near future. I do not mind starting work early in the morning or working until late at night.

I do hope you will be able to give me an interview. I can provide references from the ABC Nursery School, Dr Smith and St Martin's School.

Yours sincerely,

Sharon Singh

Sharon Singh

Links with page 57

Letter 2 – *replying to an advertisement*

21 Bishop's Lane
Southsea
Near Plymouth
Devon
PL8 1LN

Mr J. Dawson
Personnel Officer
Henshaw Services
Plymouth
Devon
PL2 2XA

22nd July, 1996

Dear Mr Dawson,

I am writing in reply to your advertisement in the Plymouth Times, 22nd July, for a trainee plumber.

I spent two weeks with your firm last October on a Work Experience programme. I worked with Mr Thomson and Mr Groves who both hoped I would apply for a job with your firm when I left school. I liked the work very much. I intend to start learning to drive in September when I am seventeen.

I have just left Tabworth School. I have always wanted to be a plumber and would very much like to take up an apprenticeship with your firm. I am strong and in good health. I do not mind working at the weekends.

I am available for interview at any time and have good references to offer.

I look forward to hearing from you.

Yours sincerely,

Chris Evans

Chris Evans

Job application

Letter 3 – *asking for an application form*

Hill View
Loughborough
Leicestershire
LE11 2EM

The Personnel Manager
Selby Services
Loughborough
Leicestershire
LE11 4GL

February 2nd 1996

Dear Sir

With reference to the post of Receptionist as advertised in
The Evening Chronicle, January 29th 1996

I would be grateful if you could send me the application form for the
above post.

Yours faithfully

Danny Tan

Danny Tan

Encl. sae

Encl. stands for enclosed or enclosures, meaning that you
have sent something with the letter.

sae stands for **s**tamped and **a**ddressed **e**nvelope.
This means that you have sent an envelope with your
address on it and a stamp, so that the firm do not have
the cost of replying to your letter.

Addressing a business envelope

Links with page 51

If you do not know the name or the job of the person you are writing to, try to give the department you want your letter to go to, e.g. Consumer Services Department.

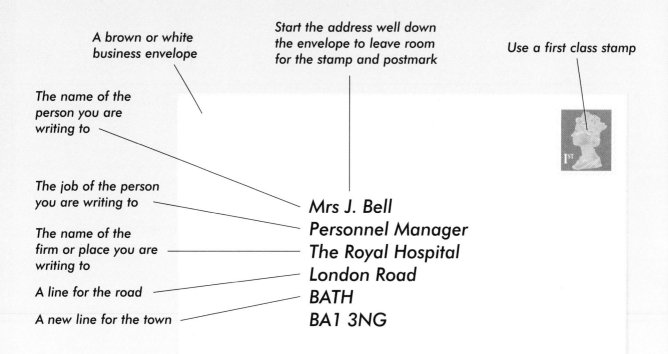

A brown or white business envelope

Start the address well down the envelope to leave room for the stamp and postmark

Use a first class stamp

The name of the person you are writing to

The job of the person you are writing to

The name of the firm or place you are writing to

A line for the road

A new line for the town

Mrs J. Bell
Personnel Manager
The Royal Hospital
London Road
BATH
BA1 3NG

Less formal letters – postcards

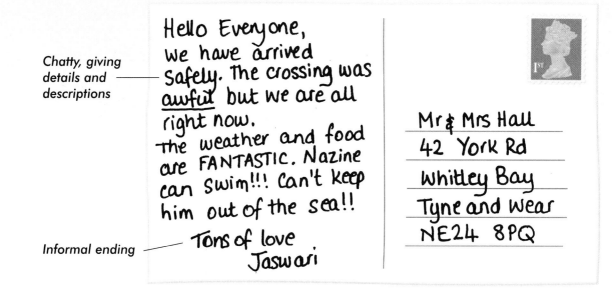

Chatty, giving details and descriptions

Informal ending

Hello Everyone,
We have arrived safely. The crossing was awful but we are all right now.
The weather and food are FANTASTIC. Nazine can swim!!! Can't keep him out of the sea!!
Tons of love
Jaswari

Mr & Mrs Hall
42 York Rd
Whitley Bay
Tyne and Wear
NE24 8PQ

Less formal letters – replying to an invitation

Jim and Keith know each other quite well.

14 Crest Road
Oxford
OX2 1PG
June 27th 1996

Dear Jim

Para 1: why you are writing —— Many thanks for inviting me to your twenty-first party.

Para 2: why you cannot go —— I'm sorry to say I won't be able to make it. Of all things, I've got to go on a two weeks' training course and I'll be miles away in Manchester on the day.

I'm so disappointed. Have a wonderful time and expect a small something in the post. (No opening it before the big day!)

informal ending —— Take care,

Keith

Letter to a close friend

Personal details, jokes, secrets

Dear Del,
Well, you can't get rid of me can you!
I just <u>had</u> to write to you. You'll never guess
what's happened now. Can you guess? I give
you three guesses. Don't CHEAT! Now, look
on the back of this page

Did you get it right? Isn't it GREAT!!

Heinemann Educational Publishers
Halley Court, Jordan Hill, Oxford OX2 8EJ
a division of Reed Educational & Professional Publishing Ltd

OXFORD MADRID ATHENS FLORENCE PRAGUE
PORTSMOUTH NH (USA) CHICAGO SÃO PAULO KUALA LUMPUR
SINGAPORE TOKYO MELBOURNE AUCKLAND NAIROBI KAMPALA
IBADAN GABORONE JOHANNESBURG MEXICO CITY

First published 1996

00 99 98 97
10 9 8 7 6 5 4 3

ISBN 0 435 10530 2

Designed and produced by Gecko Ltd, Bicester, Oxon
Illustrated by Gerry Ball, Phil Bannister, Helena Greene, Doreen McGuiness,
Pantelis Palios, Brian Smith and Gecko Ltd
Cover design by Miller Craig & Cocking
Printed and bound in Great Britain by Bath Colour Books, Glasgow

Acknowledgements

The author and publishers would like to thank the following for permission to use photographs/copyright material.

National Express Ltd for the extract from the leaflet *Coach Card*, 6; Western Morning News for the extract by
Laura Joint from *Western Morning News*, 13; James Berry for 'Coming Home on My Own' from *When I Dance*, 14;
The Controller of HMSO for an extract from the leaflet *Healthy Eating Food Sense* No 5, 16, and for reproduction of
the Birth Certificate, the design of which is Crown Copyright and the fictitious details do not relate to any living
person, 84; BBC Worldwide Publishing for 'My TV Dinner' by Mark Lewisohn from *The Radio Times*, 27/5/96, 18;
Herald & Post Newspapers for the advertising coupon from *The Gateshead Post*, 26; Gloucestershire Newspapers
Ltd for the extract from *The Citizen* 2/9/95, 28; Penguin UK for the extract from 'I Used to Live Here Once' from
Sleep It Off, Lady by Jean Rhys, 30; Rogers, Coleridge & White Ltd on behalf of Bernard MacLaverty for an extract
from 'In Bed' from *Walking the Dog and Other Stories*, copyright © Bernard MacLaverty 1994, 36, and on behalf of
Adrian Henri for 'The Bell' from *Wish You Were Here*, copyright © Adrian Henri 1990, 78; David Higham
Associates on behalf of Elizabeth Jennings for the poem 'Wasp in a Room' from *After Dark*, Oxford University
Press, 41, and on behalf of the Estate of James Herriot for the extract from *If Only They Could Talk*, Michael Joseph
Ltd, 58; Benjamin Zephaniah Associates for the extract from *Hurricane Dub* by Benjamin Zephaniah, 46;
HarperCollins *Publishers* Ltd for the extract from *Hunting Mister Heartbreak* by Jonathan Raban; Health Education
Authority for the extract from their leaflet 'Sun Know How – Shift to the Shade', 44; Barclays Bank plc for the
specimen cheque, 60; Midlands Electricity plc for their letter, 62; British Telecommunications plc for the extract
from their leaflet, 64; Littlewoods Home Shopping Group for their letter, 66; The Observer Newspaper for the
quote from *The Observer*, 68; Souvenir Press Ltd for the extract from *Where There's a Will* by Mike Brace, 74; The
Daily Mail Newspaper for the extract from *The Daily Mail* 25/2/96, 76; Angela McSeveney for 'My Crime' from
Coming Out With It, Polygon, 86; Faber & Faber Limited for the extract from *Leaving Home* by Garrison Keillor, 89.

The publishers have made every effort to trace the copyright holders, but if they have inadvertently overlooked
any, they will be pleased to make the necessary arrangements at the first opportunity.

Photographs

Apex Photo Agency Limited, 12, 13; Copyright by GAMMA, Frank Spooner Pictures, 70; Topham Picture Point, 82;
© Sally Greenhill, 82.